The Truth About Love.

The Truth About Love.

**How to really fall in love
– with your life and
everyone in it**

Conor Creighton

Gill Books

Gill Books
Hume Avenue
Park West
Dublin 12
www.gillbooks.ie
Gill Books is an imprint of M.H. Gill and Co.

978 0717194001

Designed by Marsha Swan
Edited by Neil Burkey
Proofread by Jane Rogers
Printed by ScandBook AB, Sweden
This book is typeset in Apolline.

A CIP catalogue record for this book is
available from the British Library.

5 4 3 2 1

MIX
Paper from
responsible sources
FSC® C021394

To my teacher S.N. Goenka

Contents

Part 1
Me

AN AWKWARD
FIRST DATE

Neem Karoli Baba was an Indian guru. He died in 1973. Like many holy folk, he announced he was going to die and then popped off a day or two later. Throughout his life, he performed miracle after miracle. He appeared in different locations at once. He manifested objects out of thin air. One time he pulled crisp, new money out of a burning fire. He knew things he shouldn't, what people were thinking, what they'd dreamed the night before, what was really in their heart. He was magical, truly magical.

When newcomers met Neem Karoli Baba for the first time, they'd often break down and cry. Their reaction to seeing him, this simple, bald, chubby Indian guy who wore

3

nothing more than an oversized nappy, and spoke in a kind of nasal sneer, was one of profound emotion, awe and bliss. If you go on YouTube, you'll find lots of interviews with North American boomers and Indian devotees describing their first encounter with him and, well, if they'd given birth to unicorns in a butterfly meadow beneath a double rainbow, you can't imagine their words would be as emotional.

Baba didn't teach very much. His teaching was more of a sense thing. You saw him and you got it. One glimpse and things fell into place. There are lots of people like this on the planet. They have something to them. Something more than words.

When Neem Karoli Baba did use words, however, they were very simple: Love everyone.

Your friends, your family, your neighbours, your work-mates, the people you went to school with, your new flame, your old flame, loud people, obnoxious people, boring people, landlords, clampers, spammers: love everyone.

Neem Karoli Baba was an enlightened being who lived not so long ago. By enlightened we mean that he had completed all levels of the game called 'being a human'. And his advice, after winning the game most of us struggle with every day, wasn't to buy cryptocurrency or work hard, or avoid carbs and dairy, it was simply to love everyone.

I used to believe that love was something soft. A weak thing. You might believe that too. As a boy growing up in the Irish countryside, I didn't use the word 'love' that often, not with my family, not with my friends, not even with my first girlfriends. 'You're great, you're cool, I like you, you know?' But 'I love you', the actual 'L bomb'? No, you must be mad.

To be honest, I think I was afraid of love. I was afraid to let it out. How about you? Have you let your love out this lifetime? I've dated enough through my twenties and thirties to believe that maybe we're all a little bit afraid of love. But listen to this: you are made of love.

You are made of love

Right now, wherever you are, if you get quiet and pay close attention, you can feel it rippling inside your body. Now you might call it molecules, or wavelets, or vibrations, or the pulsing creaks and groans of your old bone machine, but you could also call it love. The energy inside you is love.

It's the effort to stick a pizza in the oven when you're depressed as hell, the strength to floss your teeth when you're lonely and thinking *Who's going to kiss this mouth?* It's the power to pick up your phone and text the word SRY. It's your heart still dutifully pumping blood to your feet and hands, while you torture yourself over your lack of productivity. This is love and it's not weak, it's an enormous force.

We are trained from the youngest of ages to imagine that this force is something outside ourselves. One day your prince will come. Keep swiping. Put yourself in the window. Do all your homework and you'll get a treat. We are conditioned to believe that love is something you have to look for, you have to work for, you have to diet for. Of all the cruel messages our deeply unwell society teaches us, this is the cruellest.

But love is an inside job. We are creators of love, not discoverers of love, and until we realise that love is something that comes out of us, rather than something that comes to us, we'll never really get it, or feel it, and we'll never be able to do as Neem Karoli Baba instructed and **love everyone**.

We're living in very strange times. There is an anti-love agenda sweeping its way across our planet. You can see it in the way we're destroying nature. You can see it in the systems that govern us and the people we somehow elect into office. You can see it in our families, our marriages, how we date, how we ghost, how we tend to consume rather than celebrate each other. Thank you – next! You can see it in how we spend our time zoning out, how we are so often disempowered and small, and how we push and torture ourselves towards some twisted, unfair vision of perfection.

Perfectionism is not love. Perfectionism is self-hate in sheep's clothing.

Love everyone, said an old Indian guru, starting with you.

Love is radical

I'm a teacher. I work one on one with people who have fallen out of love with themselves. I explain to them that it's not their fault. That we all do it. That there are forces all around us on our social media, in our advertising, our governments and institutions that would deliberately keep us from loving ourselves.

They do this because if we were to love ourselves, and if we were to love everyone, then all these loveless structures would collapse. Do you think there could still be billionaires and starving people on this planet at the same time if this was a planet ruled by love? It's in the interest of the most powerful, and coincidentally most traumatised, on this planet to keep us disconnected from love.

As people, we are at our most powerful when we are generating love, and at our most disempowered when we're not.

In an often-cruel society that would have you turn against yourself and everybody around you, the most radical thing you can do is love.

Our society is becoming more compassionate. More and more people are waking up to the powerful force that is love. You might say, *Hold up, I don't see that*, but I do. When you learn to switch on your love, you not only feel more love, but you also see more love.

See love in everyone

Neem Karoli Baba said something else. He said 'See god in everyone.'

I don't believe in god. My experience of god was through a Catholic upbringing that infected me with so much shame that I used to bite my nails after masturbating. I turned against myself. Love brought me back. So if you want, you can say *see god in everyone*, but I prefer to say *see love in everyone*. It's the force, the goo, the thin, wobbly membrane that binds us all together, and truly understanding and then embracing it is the most radical thing you can do.

We're building a new society based on kinder, more heart-centred values. If you've bought this book, it means you get that too. A new society requires a direction, so:

Love everyone.

Starting with you.

BROKEN HEART REPAIRS

'Life is relationship, living is relationship. We cannot live if you and I have built a wall around ourselves and just peep over that wall occasionally.' —Jiddu Krishnamurti

When I lived in Los Angeles, I had a mechanic. His name was Sergio. Sergio didn't have his own garage. He did all his operations out of the back of his own car, which was a Toyota Camry with a large taped-up hole in the roof and a passenger door that would never open. If you had to go with him to pick up some part at a garage, you either climbed in through the driver's door, across his lunchbox and greasy water jug, or head-first through the passenger window.

As you pulled yourself inside, Sergio would whisper instructions: 'Don't touch the radio, it's loose; don't push your seat back, the hinge came off; don't breathe too much in that direction, you might blow the motor out from under the trunk.'

Sergio was Mexican, a big man, a head taller than me, who always spoke in whispers, despite the fact that most of his conversations had to compete with the sound of running engines.

And he was a phenomenal mechanic. My car at the time was an old pickup whose parts were slowly coming loose in the same way moons drift away from their planets. Each time I called him because the engine wouldn't turn, or the radio was smoking, or the bonnet had wedged itself shut, I assumed he was going to arrive with the news that there was nothing to be done, that my truck was truly a goner. And each time, within half an hour or so, he'd breathed another couple of months' life into it with the sheer force of gaffer tape and determination.

Sergio was busy too. There were times when I called him, and he'd say he couldn't be there for a week. So Sergio was making OK money. He could have bought a new car. One day, when we were driving to a garage to buy a new battery, I put my drink in the cupholder, only for the whole thing to come off in my hand. Sergio laughed. I asked him, 'Sergio, why don't you just get a new car, or at least something more fitting for a mechanic?' and Sergio said this: 'This car is like my resumé. It shows that I know a lot about broken vehicles. When people call me with their broken vehicles, they see me driving up in this piece of shit motor and they know Sergio can work with broken vehicles.' Sergio had experience with fucked-up situations.

No job too big or too small

I work with broken vehicles every day. Our minds are vehicles, and sometimes they get stuck. Sometimes they won't shut down. Sometimes they career off the road and into the dirt. Every day, in my role as a spiritual mentor – a term that makes me cringe even to write – I help people get their vehicles started again. I believe, in no uncertain terms, that the only reason I'm able to get them moving again is because I have much personal experience with fucked-up situations. When folks tell me their stories, I think of my own and offer advice based on what worked for me. My relationship history is my resumé. I've lost good friends, I spent a solid chunk of my life not really talking to my dad, and I've been engaged – rings on fingers – three times.

I hope that when you read this, you'll think to yourself, *OK, Conor's alright, he has lots of experience with broken vehicles.*

The broken vehicle I know best is myself. When I first had the idea for this book, I put that idea in the drawer where I've placed so many ideas, concluding that *It's a good one, but you're hardly qualified to write it.* The people who know me – my family, my friends and perhaps even my exes, eye-rolling so hard they might give themselves whiplash – know that I haven't had a whole lot of 'successful' relationships in my life. My love life, my family life and even some of my friendships might just as easily be described as a series of broken things held together by gaffer tape and determination.

To be honest, I've always felt a little ashamed by how many relationships I've had. As a friend once said to me when I'd come out of one relationship and landed straight into another: 'Bullets have come out of guns slower than you, Conor.'

But this is the thing: the whole point of any relationship is to create an experience in which you learn something new. If you don't mind me speaking spiritually – and I think, unless you mistook this book for another, you won't – life's lessons are attempts by a loving universe to gently, or in some cases vigorously, wake us up. Waking up means recognising what's real and what's not real.

What's not real?

Your feelings. Your thoughts. Your projections. Your identity. Your shame. Your guilt. Your sense of obligation. Your self-criticism.

What is real?

Awareness and love.

We recognise this when we meditate. The more dedicated you are to the meditation, the more you'll see. Eventually, if you keep working very hard, you'll reach a state called Nirvana. In Nirvana, a person basically dies while remaining alive. When you break up with a person, face to face, hearts beating, blood flowing, words coming out of your mouth that you practised but never imagined saying, you are also dying while staying alive. A break-up can be a lot like an out-of-body experience. Or, if you're a Buddhist, an experience of emptiness.

Blessed are the broken-hearted

'Form is emptiness and emptiness is form' is one of the oldest Zen koans. Zen koans can be a real pain in the arse. They sound like the things very clever people say to make less clever people feel miserable. But koans are not supposed to make you think you're stupid. They're just supposed to make you think.

All matter – the things we touch, love, caress, rub up against and bruise – is not matter, it's wavelets and particles, and it is empty. This is the lesson that the loving universe is trying to lead us to.

I think that bears repeating. The universe *is* loving. Most of the time we don't recognise this. In the same way that a child doesn't recognise that when its parents take the lighter out of its hands, it's not because they're hateful but because they're actually full of love. The child wails, screams and its face turns purple, but it can't see, because it still hasn't learned the lesson, that its parents are loving.

If you're wailing and screaming on account of love gone wrong right now, ask yourself, *What's the lesson in it all?* How was this experience trying to wake you up? Has a dangerous inflammable object just been taken from your hands, and you seriously want it back again?

Every encounter, every scenario, every experience has been tailor-made for you to wake up through learning something new about yourself.

If you've learned something in any relationship, then hasn't that been a successful relationship?

Relationships are places where we can get wise. And the more dramatic, the more colourful and the more varied and even troubled your relationship history (and by this I'm including every relationship, even the one you have with your neighbour), the more wisdom you'll have gathered.

Wisdom is in the air around us. It doesn't belong to you or me, it's just available for any of us at all times. If you read something on these pages and think, right, that makes sense, then it doesn't mean you're smart or I'm smart, it simply means we're breathing the same air.

Relationships are intense periods of wisdom-gathering. They're intense because they're challenging you to heal.

Love is one hell of a ride

In my mid-thirties I somehow ended up in a monastery in northern India. As much as I was curious about Buddhism, the reality of my decision to move there was that I just wanted to get off the dance floor. I was tired. I had been engaged three times in six years. Each break-up was more dramatic than the last. The final one was biblical in its drama: I found myself homeless in the Californian desert, with nothing but the constant purr of a WhatsApp argument to keep me warm at night.

Samsara is a Buddhist term for the wheel of life, the misery loops that we find ourselves in. The misery loop that I'd found myself in in that period was a series of unhappy relationships. I'd come to the decision that I wasn't able to be in a relationship, that I was so damaged, so dysfunctional that it would be better to just join a monastery and never have to deal with this aspect of my personality again. So that's what I did.

I loved monastery life. The early-morning bells, the lunchtime dahl, the silence of the meditation hall, punctured by the occasional monk fart. It was peaceful, but there was also something missing. It felt somehow too safe.

Love is risky, because it involves a journey to places that scare us.

Love often reminds me of my old car.

Sergio was a great mechanic. And he was my mechanic for another year or so. In that time he replaced my muffler when the metal overheated and peeled open on a highway. He rebuilt the A/C system after a week of 100°F days had zapped it, and he unpicked the lock on the door when a cheap copied key snapped in half inside it.

But eventually our relationship broke down too. I moved to a housesit on top of a hill near Echo Park. The hill was monstrous. You thought twice before going to the shops. 'I think you'll need to find a new mechanic,' Sergio said to me when he called over. 'I don't think my Camry is going to last much longer if it has to go up that hill each time you need me.'

SHAME ON YOU

If your body was a rental unit, and one day you couldn't feel love, you'd call the super. And the super would arrive, grumpy, the end of a roll-up on his lip, the jingle-jangle of keys around his waist, and he'd take one look at your place and say: 'Of course you can't feel the love, your pipes are all blocked up.'

Blocked up with what?

Shame.

Your brain is a highly sophisticated piece of technology with programs that govern who you think you are and how you think you're doing. And shame is pretty much the nastiest line of coding in there.

When you get to the end of this life, when you finally meet your makers – the celestial geeks of light themselves – sitting in the cocktail bar at the end of the game, and you're looking around the room and there's everyone you ever loved and hated, and they're happy to see you because there were plenty of times when it looked like you might never get this far, that smile on their face is relief.

The makers will appear, proud of you, but also eager to find out what you thought of their game, and they'll shove a glass of champagne into your still-trembling hands and ask, *So how was it?* You might want to punch them. You might also want to ask them about certain fish that got away. You might even have a question about a certain glitch you came across a number of lives back – a repeated storyline, an alien sighting, that day the sky was green instead of blue, but at the top of your list of complaints and criticisms will be shame.

'Really?', you'll say, 'You had to cripple me with that horseshit?'

That horseshit

Shame is actually the worst. The purpose of life is to love yourself just the way you are, and shame is a programming that does the exact opposite. It makes you disgusted by yourself. It makes you want to tear off your own skin. Shame disconnects us from ourselves.

Shame was like my shadow when I was growing up. I was ashamed of the house I grew up in, how it leaked in the rain, how the windows iced over on cold nights, how few gadgets we had in our kitchen. My mother told me recently about how she cried herself to sleep the first few nights we were in that home. As a baby you know when your mother's crying. As a grown man I still feel I do.

Shame followed me into my first relationships. I remember losing my virginity to an older German woman and not wanting to take off my T-shirt because she was tanned and I was, as I've always been, as I always will be, milk-bottle white.

'I'm kind of cold,' I said, on that hot July night.

The first few times I had sex I felt ashamed by my performance. How long I'd lasted. The kind of appreciative noises they made or didn't make. The funny thing is I didn't really watch porn until I was deep into my twenties. So I had no real sexual references. I was just making it up as I went along. But even without porn actors to compare myself to – and I know you shouldn't compare yourself to a porn actor because, yes, they're actors, and lighting and angles can make average things look extraordinary – I was still finding ways to chastise myself.

Shame, your ever-present shadow, meticulously inventing new and better ways to turn you against yourself.

When I look at shame and its consequences in my life, it reads like a series of taglines for movies nobody would ever want to watch.

Bright kid refuses to put his hand up in class for fear of getting it wrong.

Kid is hurt by the lack of any relationship with his father, so he pretends he has no father at all.

Dude is ashamed of his crooked teeth so he stops smiling.

A young man feels shame about his performance in bed so he avoids having sex.

Thirty-year-old doesn't go home for Christmas because of the shame of being skint around his old friends.

Aspiring meditation teacher is ashamed of appearing different, so he keeps his dream a secret.

Do the same. Write out a list of some of the things you have felt ashamed of and the consequences of indulging that shame. How that shame drove a vicious wedge between you and yourself. Now take the list and tear it up into a million pieces – or better yet, take your top off and burn it in a bin while dancing in circles and (gently) beating your chest.

Write out a list of some of the things you have felt ashamed of and the consequences of indulging that shame.

Accept yourself

When we die, we get a glimpse of this. If you spend any time with the dying, you'll notice that so much of their fatigue and weariness is related not to their body but to how they treated it over its lifetime. What they didn't do, what they did do, how they occupied their time with unimportant things that didn't, because they couldn't, bring them any of the comfort that they feel is due to them now at the end. All that bitterness, all the holding on, all that gripping to life like it was an oily fish in a bathtub, is a refusal to just admit the following: Nothing you do matters if you're not doing it with a sense of love for yourself.

When I was growing up, the worst thing you could say about another person was, 'Oh, him? He loves himself.' So when it comes to practising love for yourself, we're flooded with strong counter-reactions. It can feel as unnatural as licking a knife or staring at the sun. But even if it's not habitual, it is very natural.

So much of the work involves separating the habitual voice from the natural voice in our heads. One tip I've learned is this: Habit screams, nature whispers.

Shame is the opposite of acceptance. And I'm going to write this again in the hope that someone who will never read this book might pick it up and land on this page: Shame is the opposite of acceptance.

It's you, not me

Shame is about other people. It's not really about you.

Be alone. Deeply alone. Go and walk in some great wooded space, far from the eyes of other people, and you'll notice as you keep moving that your shame becomes so quiet, you have to call it to you like a stray dog.

When I was seventeen, I spent two months working on a mountaintop in Switzerland. There were days when I saw no one. One weekend, rain cut the valley off from the town and I didn't see another soul from Friday until Monday.

If you really knew who you are, you would never feel ashamed again.

In that time, my shame receded so far that by Sunday evening I was walking around, chopping wood, organising the larder, in hiking boots and underwear, my milk-bottle skin like a beacon on the hillside, singing De La Soul songs at the top of my voice. I felt like some great translucent, malnourished god of the Alps. Acceptance makes us all feel godlike.

Relationships are doing exactly what they're designed to do when strangers come together and share their body weirdnesses, their future fears, their particular kinks and their embarrassing dreams, and find that instead of being shamed they are accepted. This is love. You know it when you feel it because acceptance is like a reunion. You come back to all the parts of yourself that you tried to hide for so many years.

Even Buddha ghosted

A good friend of mine fosters dogs. She must have taken in about a dozen different mutts over the years. She's known at the pound, and they'll call her at all hours of the night, at weekends and even once at Christmas and say, 'Twinkles, Fido, Mr Puddles is going to be put down in six hours, would you take him for a month or so?' She's not said no yet. The dogs she houses for a month or a few months, until they get a permanent home, are usually furry messes. They piss in her plants, they chew her sofas, they scratch huge holes in the doors, they bark themselves hoarse. One time I didn't hear from her for five days because her dog had eaten the internet.

'Don't you ever get mad?', I ask her.

'I can't get mad', she says, 'look what they've come from.'

The next time you're getting mad at yourself, please look where you've come from too.

The more complicated your dating history has been, the better for you. This is important to remember. The more tears you've cried, the more lonely nights, the more desperate phone calls, desperate conversations and situations where you have found yourself thinking *Why does this only happen to me?*, the better. It's all learning. If it's been gut-wrenchingly difficult then that just means you've opted for an advanced course.

So please drop your shame. Even Buddha – who ran away from his family with no explanation to explore spirituality – ghosted someone.

THE WAR ON SINGLES

If your dating pattern is to fall for people in distress, or if you choose people whose love is assured, even if you're not sure you love them, then just like me, you probably have some dependency issues.

When you're dependent you need other people to tell you you're good, in order to feel good. Dependent people are programmed in such a way that they don't know how to generate enough self-love to sustain themselves, so they need to go out looking for it.

Dependency is not an isolated phenomenon. To be honest, unless you grew up in the wilderness with baby deer and raccoons for playmates, mountains and waterfalls as your teachers, Thich Nhat Hanh and Oprah as your parents, you're probably dependent. Ours is a dependent society. It's in our programming. But if this book is anything, it's a road map to undoing your programming, so let's look at what happens when you can't get high off your own supply.

You are enough

Dependency is an addiction, you see, and it's why most of us don't enjoy being single for long. Needy singles are the ultimate fish out of water. They are actors without a stage. Extroverts without people. They are you or me when we step out the door and realise we've forgotten our phones. They are, for the most part, really confused. And quite often, and this makes it even harder for them, they are really hot.

My dependency has led me into so many relationships that I didn't really want to be in but was just too lonely to stay away from. Can you relate?

I've always felt like I was adrift in the universe, cast away, if I didn't have at least one person who wanted me. Fievel Mousekewitz in a New York City drainpipe, drenched to the bone, singing 'Somewhere Out There', only it's

30-something me on Facebook chat to anyone who'll answer my 'long time no see' messages.

It was so important for me to know and believe that somewhere out there, somebody was thinking of me. It felt like I could only exist if I also existed in the thoughts of another.

I've stayed in touch with many of my old partners, believing that it was a sign of my great diplomacy, but that was a lie. I kept up the contact because it fed a deep desire in me to be wanted. Say my name, say my name, that kind of schtick.

We all have a bit of this, to be fair. We're all running around looking for other people to do some of the work for us. It's as if this being a human is just too much for an individual, and we need a life assistant.

It's made worse by the fact that our society tells us this is how love works. The missing piece of your life is out there, just three swipes or one speed-dating event away. Someone will complete us.

But nobody can do that. They can complement us, they can make us forget, they can throw a clean white sheet over the dusty table that is our relationship with ourselves, but in the end, we need to learn how to complete ourselves.

We need to learn how to generate love when nobody else is around to give it to us.

The most powerful gift you have is the ability to do this. Learn to do it, learn to harness your boundless capacity for love and you will change the world.

Welcome the unwelcome

Some years back, I found myself broke and unable to pay my rent. Someone suggested I house-sit. A couple of weeks later I was minding a riverside cottage in the middle of Clare, rent-free on condition that I stayed there for three months and fought off the damp that was slowly sucking the building under. I spent the first days chopping wood, walking in the hills, reading, soaking chickpeas, scraping the labels off used jars and filling them with seeds, the usual country life games.

But by week two, with enough sprouted chickpeas to feed a village, I succumbed to neediness and downloaded a dating app. Perhaps there were no houses in the vicinity, but if I knew anything about the world at large, even if there were no dwellings, there were always single people.

I set the distance to 5km – nothing. Then 10km – still nothing. I set the limit to 50km and matched with a

Canadian flight attendant, only to realise the morning after that her location was now Thailand, and that in all probability we'd matched when she was in the sky overhead.

My first response when I knew that my need for love would not be met for the foreseeable was to walk two miles to the petrol station and buy chocolate-covered peanuts and a bottle of wine. My second response was to explore it. This is the best response for any time we recognise something uncomfortable. The way we grow beyond the things that bug us is to dive into them.

Pema Chodron, the Buddhist nun, has the most beautiful advice: Welcome the unwelcome.

I credit those few months as being way more transformative than I knew at the time. Being confronted with a worldly problem that couldn't be solved with worldly solutions meant the only way out was to do nothing. Or, as folks sometimes say, surrender.

I learned to make an effort when it was just me: I'd put more flavour in my stews, I'd light candles in the evening, I'd go on morning walks where I'd come across herons perched on the bank, frozen in time. I'd watch them until my feet were numb in my boots.

I spoke to myself a lot. I said things like 'This is so tasty, thank you' when I dished up porridge. I whispered

'Looking good' when I passed the hallway mirror. And every night, lying under a duvet that was sometimes damp from all the moisture in the building, I'd say, 'Hey, you know something? You're pretty great' before falling asleep.

This is love too, you know. Simply paying close attention to you and giving gratitude for all that you do for yourself is love.

Normalise saying 'I love you' to just yourself.

There is a war on being single

The problem is that our society preys upon single people. Single is classified as somehow deficient. An incomplete action. Social media bombards single people with dating apps. Advertisers exploit you.

Landlords too. The last time I dated in Dublin, small talk included where you're from, who you know, what year you went to Australia, and whether you planned to get on the property ladder this year or next. My single friends in San Francisco face the ultimatum: move in with someone and split the rent or move out of the city they love.

To be single is to be precarious, to sit on a hot stove. It's the great waiting room of life. Folks feel uncomfortable on your behalf. What are you doing all these nights on your own? How do you cook for one? Who do you talk to? Weddings are a nightmare. Christmas back home too.

A comfort for people trapped in relationships that don't meet their needs is to believe, and to project this belief, that single folk are miserable. This is why couples often project deficiency onto single people. This deficiency infects us until it becomes an internalised narrative.

The way to break free of your narrative about being single is just to become aware that it exists. And then to remember that those in couples are often just as miserable as those who are alone.

Why being alone scares us

We believe that our happiness is dependent on things. This is how we're socialised. From the very first toy that's thrust into our hands, we're taught that our happiness is outside us, something we have to work for or find.

This reaches a kind of dizzy zenith when it comes to the notion of love. We're taught that one day we'll find someone, and this someone will take all the suffering away. This is the promise of romantic love. When you're single, the promise of romantic love nags at your being in the way that a good meal nags at your belly when you're hungry.

The problem with being single is that in a culture that doesn't encourage us to spend time with ourselves, or even to get to know ourselves, of course it's only natural that we can't imagine being happy without a significant partner. Even if you have a strong community, housemates, pets, a decent relationship with your parents, if you're not in a relationship, society will label you 'alone'.

Most of us have sad stories about being alone, but being alone provides us with a great lesson. When we're alone we can study loneliness.

I worked as a bartender for longer than I have been a meditation teacher. In bars you get to observe people at their most tender. There's as much weeping in bars as there is at funerals. At the end of the night people didn't want to go home. It was like putting small children to bed. Sometimes they'd plead with you. They loved to take the brush out of my hand and sweep the floor. Some of them would start stacking the chairs. Anything to just not go home. Some of this is alcoholism, some of it is just banter, but another part of it is loneliness. You know, because you begin to recognise the same faces, that so many of us just don't want to be left alone.

I once lived with a dog like this. If you left him alone in the house, he would scratch the door and chew the carpet and work himself into a blind frenzy. I remember at the time thinking how traumatised the poor thing was, until I was reminded of how I couldn't spend a night alone without a bottle of wine, a bar of chocolate, Netflix, and two or three WhatsApp chats with people rightly suspicious of my motives for contacting them after years of radio silence.

Our culture conditions us to always look for the end of suffering in things. In this culture people are also things. We consume each other like the hung-over consume Solpadeine.

Our attraction towards relationships is our attempt to finally find a product that will make us feel whole, that will make the shifting ground beneath us solid. But as anyone who's ever loved knows, the solidity we find in relationships, like the future and like the past, is not real.

'Love you till the day I die' is often not the end of anxiety but rather the beginning of it. All we ever have is this present. The difficulty with being single is actually just a difficulty being with yourself. Existence, simply, is loaded with pain.

I'd never have meditated or picked up a spiritual book or taken myself off to India, where I counted more sick days than not-sick days, if it hadn't been for this pain. My pain was an inability to generate my own love. My inability to be okay being single.

Cultivate your awareness

At the heart of our fear of being single is the problem of being alive. Buddha recognised this problem, and his solution to it was to find enlightenment. When it comes to our personal journeys, don't you think it's a great comfort to realise that Buddha was also miserable before he did the work?

Enlightenment for Buddha was the recognition that everything was in a state of constant flux, constant change, that nothing had solidity, there were no handrails, no safe structures, and the only way to coexist in this bouncy castle of a reality was to not look for what wasn't there.

Instead of playing the game, he decided to step out of the circle. Rather than be the star of the movie, he decided to climb into an audience seat and observe it instead. We get to do that if we want. We get to observe discomfort rather than suffer discomfort.

The next great leap for humankind, and to be honest, it'll happen even if we don't want it to, might be when we begin to experience our lives with a playful curiosity rather than personal fatalism.

To be curious simply means to be aware.

Awareness is what we cultivate when we let go of our stories. Our stories are the programming that governs our lives. You know what I'm talking about. Perhaps your story is that you think you're ugly, or that you're a terrible lover, or, god forbid, that you're a terrible person.

These are our stories. To be honest, they're kind of fucked. Seeing through the illusion of our stories is the goal of our spiritual work and the whole point of this book. For you and for me.

Our stories

At the risk of losing half of the readers in a sentence, our world is a bit like the Matrix, in the movie of the same name. The Matrix is an illusionary world maintained by false perceptions. When Morpheus first brings Neo out onto the rooftop, he instructs him: 'Let it all go, Neo. Fear. Doubt. Disbelief. Free your mind.'

He might have been echoing the great Thai Buddhist monk Ajahn Chah: 'If you let go a little, you will have a little peace. If you let go a lot, you will have a lot of peace.'

The world we perceive is a story. If your story is a nightmare, it might be some comfort to you to know that you can let it all go.

Buddha was a normal man with an extraordinary capacity to let go. He let go so much he got completely free. If he can do it, you can too. Buddha understood that his suffering was his story. Your story, that you are unlovable, unsuccessful, undesirable and so on, is the cause of your suffering too.

Suffering is not the point of life, but suffering is to life what a white beard is to Santa Claus. If your life is completely free of suffering, check the manufacturer's details, as you might just have been sold a fake.

The suffering is what brings us eventually to self-inquiry. If it wasn't there, we'd do dull jobs, eat the same meals and watch *Friends* reruns each evening for the rest of our days and be perfectly satisfied. But we're seldom satisfied. If we were, we'd never suffer and we'd never question things.

Buddha taught suffering and the end of suffering. He taught suffering first because unless you can recognise suffering you won't put in the work to change. So let's talk about it.

Suffering occurs when our realities are not what we want them to be. If you look at your own life you can probably list as many as ten examples, from today alone – from this morning alone – of moments when your life was not how you wanted it to be.

You wake up and for some reason you're not feeling as energised as you hoped you'd be. You go to the fridge, and the oat milk – the oat milk that you spent a decent amount of money on – is not quite empty, but there is not quite enough to make your coffee taste smooth like coffee should. An email comes in with a rejection letter from a job you'd applied for. You check your social media, and instead of your usual 50 likes, you only got 40. You call your partner, and instead of being excited to hear your voice, they're stressed and rush you off the phone. Meanwhile, your digestion system, a system that is so slick, so seamless, so regular that you can set your phone by it, is off. It's getting on for lunch and you still haven't digested last night's curry.

If you recognise the sequence playing out above, and you can relate, perhaps you too can see the dull buzz of suffering in your own life. This isn't unique. We're all just tender, loving beings who want to be happy.

The remedy we've been sold for the longest of times is that our only way to happiness, and the end of suffering, is in the arms of somehow who loves us.

Generate your own love

In the future we'll all be more or less single in spirit. We'll commit to our own personal journey and along the way we'll find partners who are willing to split the fare, and because of this our relationships will be smoother, because our expectations will be lower. In this model our relationships will last for ever.

In the future we will be healed people who love without conditions, because in the future when we feel ourselves falling, we won't look to other people to save us; we'll look to ourselves.

Love will be no longer a coping mechanism but a celebration of the joy of being complete in ourselves. Our love will come from a place of generosity, not a need to consume others.

It's going to be a great party. You should come.

Part 2
It

WHAT IS LOVE
ACTUALLY?

My dad grew up in Belfast. Self-help was not a big theme in the seventies in Northern Ireland. My dad didn't get taught about his emotions, but that didn't stop him learning. I inherited his hair, his humour and his tendency towards melancholy, and we talk about it. We have long, sprawling conversations about sadness over Facetime that feel like puzzle-solving. We are evolving. We're maturing. People are getting better and more loving. If you want to, you can see love everywhere.

When you can attune yourself to the vibration of love, the positive voices rise up like a choir. That's a very spiritual thing to say. But it's also scientific. Human beings are surrounded by electromagnetic fields. Your body can radiate love if you want it to. Much like the way kids with speakers can take over a train carriage, you, with just your simple beating heart, can fill up any space you enter.

If you've grown up with religion, you might not equate love with spirituality. In that case, your idea of spirituality might be severity, and discipline, and men giving orders. Spirituality is not really about anyone else but you. It's personal. It is a non-hierarchical exploration of the mysteries of your own existence, and despite what many charismatic opportunists have claimed throughout history, you are the only authority you need to consult when it comes to yourself.

The acid test of whether something or someone is truly spiritual or not is to feel if it's loving. There is no spirituality without love.

As a species we are slowly learning to be more loving. As an assorted interconnected people, with different opinions, preferences and interpretations of what is salty, and what is not salty enough, we're learning, as indeed each individual must learn, that love is more important than we thought.

What love is not

People are strange, Charles Bukowski wrote. They are constantly angered by trivial things, but on a major matter like totally wasting their lives, they hardly seem to notice.

On a major matter like love, it's not that we hardly seem to notice, but we don't fully explore it. We search for love, we pine for love, we get annoyed by those who rub it in our face that they have found love, but what is love actually? It's a question we could do with asking ourselves more often.

For the majority of us, and in the majority of cases, what we take love to be is completely wrong.

M. Scott Peck wrote a very important book in 1978 called *The Road Less Travelled*. It was a self-help book in my dad's era. In it he describes love as the will to extend one's self for the purpose of nurturing one's own or another's spiritual growth. Love is not about how you feel, or what you might receive; it's about what you do and the purity of your intention. What we in our lives take to be love is often actually the opposite.

Think of the following sentences. Maybe you've heard them before. Maybe you've used them before. They're all, more or less, used in the name of love.

If you leave me, I won't survive.

Don't talk back to me, I'm your parent.

I do everything for you.

You have to come to my party. I won't hear any excuses.

I love you more than you love me.

If I'd known you'd leave me I'd never have cared so much.

I'd love you more if you listened to me.

The love that we imagine exists in relationships, friendships and our families is often based on conditions and rules and manipulation and control and future payoffs. This isn't love.

When you think back on all the love you've known, how much of it really was true, and how much of it was a means to control and influence you?

When couples break up, there's often a feeling of resentment for giving so much. That the effort made wasn't commensurate with the result. If we truly loved the people we say we love, then wouldn't we only care about their happiness, even beyond the relationship? It's tough to swallow, but if I love my partner and they leave me for their own personal growth, even if that growth is with someone else, then if I'm angry with them, can I really say I love them or that I ever loved them?

Families are often united by a sense of obligation and guilt and a desire to be accepted and understood. How often do we as children make decisions to avoid upsetting our parents, and how often do parents project their own wishes, desires and fears upon us?

At least once a week, I talk to someone who has found themselves in the wrong place in life. They're doing a job, playing a role, leading relationships that neither stir their soul, excite them nor align with their values.

'Why are you doing this?'

'I just wanted to make my parents proud.'

'Wasn't that a given?'

'I don't know. I always felt that I wasn't enough.'

'Do you think that's love?'

'Well, they said they loved me.'

Look at our friendships, the people we choose rather than the families we're hurled into. These are the people we look to for acceptance and understanding when we can't get it at home.

But friendships, many friendships, are places of censorship, bullying, competition and dishonesty, where nobody wants to be truly vulnerable in case they are too much, too heavy, too open, too much of a buzzkill.

If your friends truly loved you, wouldn't they love you however you showed up, and whatever you said? Wouldn't friendship be a place where you could experiment and grow and not face rigorous inspection?

I have lived in a few countries. I've started over again on at least five different occasions. Almost every time I left, I wasn't sick of the place so much as tired of playing a role in front of my friends.

You might be reading this in the exact same position. You might find yourself embroiled in many relationships where you can't be you, you can't change, you can't grow.

Love is spiritual growth

Right now, you're reading a spiritual book. This book, if I've done my job properly, will nurture your spiritual growth. So if you're reading a book like this, and as long as you're doing it voluntarily, and not because your partner has glued it to your bare hands, you're showing love to yourself. But let's move beyond you.

Think for a second of all the people you love. Write their names in the margin of the book if you like. It's yours now, I won't take offence. How often do you think about their spiritual growth? How often do you really consider their potential and their expansion as a mysterious fellow human instead of what you might need from them, or what they might do for you?

Think for a second of all the people you love. Write their names in the margin of the book if you like.

We have a tendency to consume people. We love them for what they do for us. This isn't love. Love flows out of you with no expectation. When love is interpreted as something that comes to us, then it's easy to see why we say things like 'I love Friday,' or 'I love kimchi,' or 'I love the sunshine.' But really, what have you ever done for the sun?

Love is the force that got us out of the water and onto the land. It's what made us raise our arms and walk on two legs. Love is the reason we have the internet, and, indirectly, spam, but also hours of footage of happy rescue animals. Love is not a passive consumption, it's an active, bustling, nourishing energy. Love is work. It's watering a flower rather than plucking it until it eventually dies.

Too often we confuse love with entertainment. This cheapens love. Love is a superpower. A tub of Ben & Jerry's might be the best thing you can eat off your belly on a lonely Monday, but that's not love.

The people who hurt us

Buddha was an expert on love. He said, 'If you truly loved yourself, you'd never hurt another.'

I'm sorry, but love means attempting to nurture the spiritual growth of the bastards too.

The people who inflict hurt are the people who know love least. Hate, fear, jealousy and sadness are all mental states that arise when we are feeling furthest from love. These mental states are traps, temporary prisons that we can't manage to leave.

Think about the last time you were in a mood. Maybe you're in one right now. It can feel like you've been locked down, right? It can feel unfair. Our spiritual growth is our freedom from moods.

Buddha was locked up himself. The guy was depressed and miserable, so he left home in search of techniques to end his suffering. After trying everything, he discovered a thing called the middle way. The middle way is a radical acceptance of our experience.

You are in a human body with a brain, and the habit pattern of the brain is to seek pleasure and avoid pain. There's nothing wrong with that, except the world is not made by Walt Disney. The world is very fairly divided into highs and lows. Buddhists describe it as 10,000 joys and 10,000 sorrows. How's your tally so far?

Sit with your thoughts

Our way of living with the unending ping-pong game between joy and sorrow is to remain intensely present with your experience. When we are present, we are not bounced up and down all the time. Presence is freedom.

Right now, just place this book in your lap and bring a little presence to your thoughts.

Our thoughts are a reflection of our environment. They are largely negative, because their purpose is not to make you feel at ease, or content, or even good about yourself. Your thoughts have been designed to keep you alive. They decided, your thoughts I mean, that the best way to keep you alive is to keep you on your toes: stressed, worried, bubbling up with fear.

By getting really present with our thoughts, we can notice that their pattern is to come and go, come and go, come and go. They are not real. Our thoughts are the building blocks of the stories that shape our lives, but if we watch them, if we get really present, we see that our stories, the things we so dearly hold on to, have no substance to them.

The first time I went on a ten-day silent meditation retreat, I arrived brimming with hateful thoughts for an ex-girlfriend. And man, did I ever have my reasons. She promised to love me for ever, and then inexplicably stopped. She told me I was the last man she'd ever be with, and then left me for someone else. She promised to be in my life for ever, to grow old with me, to have our children, to plant trees and watch them grow in our garden, and now I was blocked from all her social media accounts, and she wouldn't give me back my white denim jacket.

I arrived at the meditation retreat drowning in justified anger. Buddha described anger as a blade covered in honey. It feels so good, but ultimately it destroys you. As I meditated, day after day, I slowly became more and more present. As you become more present, something amazing happens: you begin to see the reality as it is, you begin to see how unreal your stories are, and you begin to take responsibility for your own life. By day five I was no longer angry at my ex, and I felt free.

The whole reason we read books like this is to get free. The freedom that I'm talking about is freedom from our thoughts and from our stories.

Let go of fear

For love to be real, it also needs to be free. Free from conditions. If we look at the conditions we bring into our relationships, we can see that they're attempts to control other people. Do we really want to love the people we claim to love, or do we want some power over them?

Where love rules, there is no will to power, and where power predominates, there love is lacking. Carl Jung said this. If you want love to rule, you have to stop controlling it, and you have to stop controlling people.

Nearly all the work we encounter in relationships is letting go of our need for control. Nearly all the work we encounter in our lives is also letting go of control. Life is always moving. Any attempt to control it is as frustrating and useless as trying to hold back the tide. But we do it all the same. We're scared, that's why. Our brains are fragile, highly sensitive, projecting devices that create our realities based on impressions and memories. The collective memory of the human race is one of fear.

We are not well. As people and as a planet. This is clear. We've lost our connection to ourselves. We have forgotten who we are. If we really knew who we were there'd be no scarcity or anxiety or depression on this planet. Earth would be a type of paradise powered by the hum of our collective good vibrations.

Love is our way of remembering who we are. Love is spiritual growth. Right now you're growing. As you read these pages, I hope the world beyond this book becomes less and less scary. I hope love becomes less scary.

This is the thing about scary places: fear can't exist where there is love. We live in a world where fear is used to keep us stuck, but our world is actually loving.

In moments of crisis we spring to each other's rescue. The human race might be complacent and solipsistic and troubled, but nobody will convince me that we're not loving and kind and heroic too.

We're living through an incredibly precarious time. The planet is in rag order. Our sense of community is bigger than it's ever been, but more fractious than it's ever been too. There are people profiting from promoting a loveless agenda and encouraging radical individualism, an atomised society connected through messaging services and cartoon hearts. Love has been diluted and repackaged as something rare and fleeting and as something we consume.

Real love, the dormant force at the pit of your stomach, is the solution to all our problems right now. In a world infused with love, we feel connected to and cared for by everyone we meet.

Love is a war cry

Buddha said some more things about love.

> Conquer anger with non-anger. Conquer badness with goodness. Conquer meanness with generosity. Conquer dishonesty with truth. Radiate boundless love towards the entire world.

If you, like me, grew up with the idea that love was somehow soft, that love was weak, or that love was perhaps not so important, then it might help to read that last quote a few times aloud to yourself. Old Buddha, the most peaceful little man on the planet, a guy who would look at you and you'd melt – four times he uses the word 'conquer'.

This is a beautiful, sweet, tender quote, but it's also, and don't let this pass you by, a war cry.

THE HEAD vs THE HEART

'If you're looking for something that is everywhere, you don't need travel to get there; you need love.' — St Augustine

For a huge part of my life I was anti-spirituality. Happy-clappy people: I hated them. Incense: I wouldn't even burn it. And silence, sweet, faultless silence, I drowned out with news radio, beats, loud distorted guitars, endless chatter. I spent most of my life feeling resentment towards spiritual folk in the same way people on the edge of the dance floor turn their noses up at those in the centre.

I can remember dating a meditator once when I was just 23, by accident really – we were neighbours. I ran into her in the stairwell, bringing a month's worth of pizza boxes down to the bins.

We were both living in a building in Naples. She lived above me, and sometimes I'd come upstairs to read and find her sitting in a complicated position on the terrace.

'What's that?', I'd say.

'Half lotus.'

'Half-mad,' I'd say under my breath. 'Did the aliens have any messages for you this morning?'

'I'm not talking to aliens, I'm listening to myself.'

I don't know why she dated me, to be honest, because I was an idiot back then. Proximity probably played a role in it. How convenient is it to get your loving next door?

She had a morning meditation practice and an evening ritual, where she'd burn palo santo sticks and line up her crystals in the fading sunlight and write out affirmations in her journal like they were lines given to her by a schoolteacher.

I'd watch her and feel strange emotions inside me that I couldn't interpret, so I labelled them as anger. If you are disconnected from yourself, if you don't listen to yourself often, you might also label the longings, the sadness and the stirrings in your belly as anger.

We broke up as soon as she saw that I was not to be saved. We're still in touch. I wrote to her on the same day that I bought my very first crystal, when I was about 37. It's a black tourmaline. To be honest, it doesn't even look like a crystal. I wear it on a string round my neck and most folk would think it's one of those Māori necklaces from the 1990s. Baby steps.

I wrote her and apologised for being such a little shit back in the day. This is what I said:

> *I understand now that the antagonistic feelings in me were just a longing for some form of spiritual feeding. I was all up in my head, projecting anger onto everything. Sorry.*
>
> *PS: I write affirmations too now. They cover the walls of my home like to-do lists. My favourite one is this:*
>
> *I love myself for who I am.*

How to get spiritualised

You have spiritual needs. We all do. We're not automatons. Not yet anyway.

Becoming spiritual is simply about listening to what's going on on the inside. It's about getting out of your head and into your heart. You don't need to invest in crystals or incense, or even write out affirmations, but if you want to, and if nobody is within earshot, how about this:

Say the following out loud, three or four
times: I love myself for who I am.

If you don't like what you see outside you, look inside
yourself instead. The world is not flooding towards you;
instead it's pouring out of you. When you pay very close
attention, you can see the whole show coming to life inside
your mind. You're not a simple actor, as you might have
believed, you're the whole theatre.

Our minds create the world around us. And yet our
heads are unreliable. That's where thoughts exist, and our
thoughts don't know shit about love. Our thoughts are
like the lobbyists for our conditioning. Negative, repetitive
absorbers of the environments and culture around us. You
will run into shame, guilt, obligation and judgement up
there, but you won't encounter love.

If I could go back in time and meet the younger version
of me, in all the bars and shared homes and bedrooms he
found himself in, I'd say, *Buddy, drink some water now and*
again, but also don't think so much, get out of your head and feel
a little more.

There is an old Indian expression that a knife can't cut
itself. It means that what you are can't be fully perceived

by you. This frustrates the head. Its job is to make sense of things, and when it can't, it invents something. The reason we feel less than, small and disempowered, is because our brain, in its attempts to understand us, has failed, and come up with a shitty alternative.

Learning to love means learning to let go of the need to define yourself, and embracing the concept that you are a continually unfolding process that can only be experienced and felt.

We feel with the heart.

Ramana Maharshi, the Indian guru, used to say that someone who goes and lives in a cave and spends their entire lives purifying themselves has done more for all humanity than someone who has established great charities all over the world. Meaning, if you can work on yourself, if you can explore all your delusions and neuroses and arrive at a place of acceptance, you will have done more for the world than if you had dedicated your life to service to the world.

That is hard to wrap your head around. As are a lot of the things said by bona fide holy people. When they talk, what they say is mostly an invitation, not to believe it, but to get curious about it yourself.

Like love, like sex, like your first grey hair, words can hint at but can't prepare you for the experience. At a micro level, I know that the world I encounter post-meditation is a kinder, milder place than before I've closed my eyes, and therefore it does incline me to meditate more when I notice that the world feels tighter, or more dramatic.

Your head is a helicopter parent

So what's up with our heads, and why do they make connection, love, trust and finding the perfect message to send someone after a cute first date so hard?

Our minds are programmed for negativity – not to torture us, but to keep us alive. Worry, stress, self-criticism, wanting and comparison are all ways our brains show us love.

It is love, but it's a love you don't need.

I have a friend who grew up with a stepbrother who was 15 years older than him. This stepbrother tried to protect him from the world by making him scared of it.

'He used to tell me things – that if I masturbated, my dick would fall off. Or if I drank alcohol, I would immediately become an alcoholic. He warned me about women too. He said crazy things, like they were incapable of love, and you couldn't trust any of them, and because he was my older brother and I looked up to him, I believed every word of it and did what he said. I didn't touch myself, or anyone else, or even alcohol, until I was in my early twenties.'

'And then what?'

'I went absolutely nuts … I became addicted to sex and booze and wound up in rehab. In rehab I learned that my brother had been trying to show me love, but in the wrong way.'

Your brain is trying to love you in the wrong way too. It shows you love by being protective and scaremongering to the point of suffocation. It scares us into never trying anything, so we won't have to suffer the pain of failure. But your brain doesn't know who you really are. Your heart does. In your heart there's no such thing as failure.

Our programming exists in our brains. Our programming is the puppet strings dragging us back into patterns and habits and cycles. It's what keeps us trapped. Buddha described his own programming as a house. On the day of his enlightenment, he spoke to his programming.

> O house builder, you have been seen;
> You shall not build the house again.
> Your rafters have been broken up,
> Your ridgepole is demolished too.
> My mind has now attained the unformed Nirvana
> And reached the end of every sort of craving.

Your programming is a cowboy builder. They keep building a house on your perfectly fine empty lot. Each time you tear it down, they sneak back in the night and rebuild it. You tear it down again. They build it right back up. Your house is your identity, and your identity is the one thing keeping you from living a life of love.

Your heart knows best

Nirvana means ultimate reality. It translates as 'blowing out'. Blowing out all the delusions of your mind and recognising the ultimate reality: that we are made of love.

When we live from the head, we construct these small identities that constantly need to be maintained. I like this person, I like this colour, I don't like this talk, I don't like this touch and so on and so on. It's a system that is maintained by wanting, by craving. It's why when you're with one person you want to be with another. And when you're with another you want to go back to the first person again.

This house builder, this identity, it's the reason we're always exhausted. We need to learn how to blow it out. Jiddu Krishnamurti said this: 'There is great happiness in not being something.' Think about that. We live in a society obsessed with making a name for yourself, prestige, getting a bunch of likes for your photo that, with all those filters, isn't really you any more anyway, is it?

All the wisest people who have walked this earth have talked about the joy of being nobody.

Being nobody is living from the heart. Living from the heart means trusting in your true self rather than the false identity created in your head. It's scary. To live from your heart means to always be on thin ice, tossed from the nest, diving into the unknown with no home, no fixed identity, no false sense of security. No wonder our heads don't buy into this. Our head is the seat of fear, and our heart is the motor of love.

If your dreams don't scare you, they're not big enough

I believe that we are on the edge of a great revolution for humankind. So much is up for grabs. Our heads, and our programming, will only bring us so far. The future is all about the heart.

So before you go on, just put this book down and see if you can feel it. And as you feel it, as you sense your heart inside your chest, you might also become aware of the identity in your head, the disempowered voices that are afraid of your expansion. Your thoughts don't hate you.

They just don't know who you really are. But you do. Deep
down you have an inkling. That's why you've read so far.

*Get very quiet and very still. Tune into
the sound of your heart beating against
your chest. Can you hear it? Can you feel
it? If your heart could speak right now,
what would it say to you?*

Belief is walking a tightrope. Too far left and you fall
into hyperbolic superstition and might not leave your home
when the planets are misaligned. Too far right and you
become a radical reductionist and fail to see the mystery in
anything. A mature spirituality is a spirituality with balance.
We might be right, but we might also be wrong.

In Zen Buddhism they teach the beauty of maintaining a 'don't know mind'. As you read this book, I'd encourage you to take everything with a pinch of salt. What do I
know, right? You're on your own path. You have to walk it
yourself. You get to decide what is good for you, and this is
true empowerment.

Everything is real, but nothing is literal. Your internal
experience is all that counts. Don't overthink it.

WHY WE GET
LOVE WRONG

*'If we're committed to comfort at any
cost, as soon as we come up against
the slightest edge of pain, we're going to
run; we'll never know what's beyond that
particular barrier or wall or fearful thing.'*
—Pema Chodron

A common misbelief that humans have is that the way to
find lasting happiness is to avoid pain and discomfort. This
sets us up terribly for all relationships. It's not that love hurts
extraordinarily, it's just that we don't expect it to hurt at all,
and when it does, the feeling of disappointment, the feeling
of betrayal, is often worse than what actually happened.

We're told that love should be easy, but nothing on this planet is really easy, so why would the most transformative, mysterious and occasionally terrifying emotion fall into that category?

Giving and receiving love are two of the hardest things we ever learn to do. It takes time. It takes practice. It takes experience. Love is a square peg, but our heads are round holes. It might take you a lifetime, or many lifetimes, to learn this.

As the Taoist sage Chuang Tzu said: 'When you open your heart, you get life's ten thousand sorrows, and ten thousand joys.' It's not personal. It just is what it is.

Chuang Tzu also said this: 'Flow with whatever is happening and let your mind be free.'

If I had met Chuang Tzu in a bar when I was in my twenties, if he'd seen me at the counter, drinking a beer, ripping into a beer mat, in deep anguish over whatever current relationship I was in, and he'd come up to me and placed a cold hand on my shoulder and said, 'Flow, Conor, just flow', then Chuang Tzu might have had a pint over his head.

Relationships aren't meant to be easy

Our relationships, at least when we're younger, are not meant to be easy. They're custom-designed to make us suffer in just the right way necessary for us to grow and wake up, the hope being that finally, one day, if luck is on your side, you'll drop enough of your notions, expectations, childish demands and conditioning, and realise one of the hardest tasks on the planet: living in harmony with someone else.

Once we can get used to this idea, once we realise that trying to make it work is about as tough as bringing the ring to Mordor, we'll begin to understand what we're really taking on the next time we make the ambitious and naïve decision to fall in love.

I have an Italian friend called Luca. Luca is bound by a different kind of wisdom from mine. When I suggest we get takeout coffee and go for a walk, he'll say things like, 'Conor, in Italy only horses drink standing up'. His wisdom is Italian, and he's grown up with a gigantic lexicon of Italian expressions; he can use them at all times and in all situations. He's a human Wikipedia of sage soundbites. This is one:

*Se non hai mai pianto, i tuoi occhi
non possono essere belli.*

*If you've never cried, your eyes
cannot be beautiful.*

I know Luca's cried a lot. I met him on the day his girlfriend of seven years told him it was over and she was getting back with her ex.

Luca has beautiful eyes. They're beautiful because they've been polished by many tears. Buddha, if he'd been born in Ravenna instead of northern India, might have come out with something similar.

Expecting our lives and our relationships to be easy misses the point of life altogether. Our life is like a course we've signed up for. It's a fully immersive course with no breaks, no time-outs, no winter or summer holidays and plenty of tests. These tests will feel unpredictable at first. Some years will go by like a personal attack. *Really? Again? But I just completed a test yesterday!* But as you get to know the course better, you'll understand that every moment is a test, and the constant testing won't bother you in the same way. If you manage to become a mature student of life, you'll even begin to relish the testing. Shit will hit the fan and you'll smile and think to yourself, *Damn, I'm really getting my money's worth this time around.*

If your life has been difficult, you can actually take that as a compliment. It's a sign that you are on an advanced course. Only folks who've done a lot of work get to sit advanced courses. If this sounds like you, please

don't lose heart. You were born for this. You might even
have chosen it.

'We are not human beings having a spiritual experience; we are spiritual beings having a human experience,'
said Pierre Teilhard de Chardin.

Many highly spiritual people have spoken about the
idea that we are gods in human bodies. Do you ever get
that feeling that you know more than you allow yourself to
know? That your limits are kind of an illusion? According
to many great spiritual people, we actually know everything and are capable of anything. We are gods.

Mooji is a Jamaican teacher. He used to sell incense
sticks in Camden Market in London, and then all of a
sudden people started coming to him for advice. They
stopped buying his incense. A following grew around him,
and he moved to Portugal and built a centre for healing.

Mooji said this:

> You are not here by accident.
> This form is just a costume for a while.
> But the one who is behind the costume,
> this one is eternal. You must know this.
> If you know this and trust this,
> you don't have to worry about anything.

So we are eternal. We are an energy. Energy can't be destroyed, it can only be transformed. We are an eternal energy that comes to earth in order to learn some tough lessons about existence.

You're right where you're meant to be

You were born here because you have certain work to do that involves the suffering you do, the kinds of situations you find yourself in. This is your curriculum. It's not an error. Where you are now, with all your neuroses and your problems, you're sitting in just the right place. Imagine that.

Think about your own life right now and think about the decision you might have made before you got here. Think, if you can, about the decision you might have made before you entered into your mamma's womb.

In this life I'll be incredibly wealthy so I can truly learn how power corrupts.

In this life I'll be a single parent with three children so I can understand compassion.

In this life I'll be the outsider in the community, so I'll get to know how important it is to love yourself.

*In this life I'll suffer so much that the only path
to healing will be opening my heart further than I
imagined possible.*

Ram Dass was hit with a stroke about 15 years before he died. It meant that this great speaker, this lover of the stage, slowly lost the ability to speak. In the end he required help feeding, bathing, pooping, getting into bed – 10,000 joys and 10,000 sorrows much?

He said this about his illness:

What a gift the stroke has given me, to finally learn that I don't have to renounce my humanity in order to be spiritual — that I can be both witness and participant, both eternal spirit and aging body.

That's rather incredible. Maybe you're reading this and thinking, *Not me, I couldn't have that perspective*, but if one of us can, we all can. That's the truth.

No mud, no lotus

If our life does not go to plan, we tend to take it personally. We tend to blame ourselves for it. We tend not to recognise that the point of challenges is not to defeat you, but to facilitate your growth. We forget that maybe we chose the life we're living right now.

Buddha used to tell a story about four horses: the excellent horse, the good horse, the poor horse and the really bad horse.

The excellent horse needs no commands from the rider. It just gets it naturally. No whip, no sugar cubes, nothing. You sit on its back and it goes, perfectly. The good horse needs a bit more encouragement. The poor horse, well that needs a lot of encouragement and much training, and the really bad horse, Christ, the really bad horse is practically hopeless. The really bad horse won't budge, won't even get to its feet, wouldn't move if it was paid.

When it comes to spirituality, what type of horse are you?

According to Buddha, in the end the best horse was the really bad horse, because in order for this horse to move it has to be thoroughly convinced that it's worth it.

If your path to reading a book like this and your path to change has involved sugar cubes, pestering and maybe even some use of the whip, then you won't be deterred. Struggle will, in the long run, make you more determined.

No mud, no lotus, as Thich Nhat Hanh said. And there's nothing muddier than a relationship.

When I scan the battlefields of my previous relationships, the hardest part to swallow was never the arguments – it was the disheartenment.

Dis-heart-enment

It sounds like a surgical procedure. *Doctor, stop talking and just remove the bloody thing!*

Luca, always on hand with the deep Italian wisdom, would say that suffering is to love what a headache is to wine.

The point of life and indeed the point of relationships is not to suffer; the point is to recognise when we are suffering, and to learn.

Everyone I have ever met carries echoes of previous relationships. If you can recognise these patterns, it's a sign that you're learning. For most of my life, I wouldn't have recognised a pattern if it had climbed into bed beside me and stuck its tongue in my ear. I thought, as most of us do, that I was simply unlucky in love.

I didn't know that I had a choice. You might not know that either. But when you can begin to see that it's your mind that's creating the world, you also get to see that, rather than being a victim of life, you actually have all the power.

Love is not blind

Yogacara is an ancient theory from India. It predates neuroscience by a couple of thousand years. It claims that our sense of the world – i.e. how the world is served to us day in, day out – is dependent upon past and present conditioning. Another word for conditioning is 'culture'. What we know is what we expect.

Modern neuroscience explains Yogacara as a bunch of synapses and neurotransmitters creating your reality based upon your own particular psychological makeup, aka a simulator.

Anil Seth, a professor of cognitive neuroscience, describes the mind as a 'highly evolved prediction machine … constantly hallucinating the world and the self'.

We perceive life through the simulator of our thoughts. If you believe in your thoughts, then you have no freedom when it comes to who you fall in love with. Someone will come along, and the thought will appear: this is my type. And because we don't question these thoughts, we'll find ourselves always in the same relationships.

Love is not blind; it's actually a hallucination.

This is why our experience of love can be so irritating. Love for many of us – this chump included – can be like playing with fire. We need breaks from love. We turn our back on love. We hope that we won't fall in love. We express it on dates: I'd rather not have something serious. I'm not looking for love. *Oh, is that love? Thanks, but I'll pass.* Love for some appears to have the value of an experience you wouldn't wish upon your worst enemy.

Buddhists describe the world we live in as 10,000 joys and 10,000 sorrows. Jon Kabat-Zinn, the meditation teacher, describes life as treacherous waves. How do we deal with them? We learn to surf.

Surfing the waves of life means accepting everything and remembering that you are an eternal source of energy that creates the world around you. Love included.

Don't be afraid of love

If the world seems like a loveless place, maybe that's not always the world's fault – maybe it's ours. If we can reconnect to our own loving presence as individuals, then collectively we will change the world.

Instead of waiting for love, we'll just make it.

There is an anti-love agenda embedded in our markets, our schools, our technologies, our workplaces, our sports, our religions and even our cultural institutions. Instead of connecting us, these places and systems encourage isolation, competition and disconnection. They make us feel like we're victims. This chapter is all about reminding you that you're not a victim – in fact you might just be the most powerful force in the universe.

When the person you're messaging has left you on read for two days and you can't decide whether this merits a follow-up or a ghosting, thinking about this helps.

You're not small and hoping to one day be big; you're big and seeing what it's like to be small.

There is an ultimate truth pertaining to our reality. This ultimate truth is that we are not who we think or even feel we are. Our bodies are nothing more than wavelets and particles suspended, created and re-created in micro-seconds. The same is true of our world. It emanates from us. Our lives are like conveyor belts inventing themselves before our eyes. This is ultimate truth. Buddha didn't discover this. There were many traditions in India and throughout the world that knew this long before he did. Buddha's contribution to our knowledge of ultimate truth was to create a pathway to experience it. The pathway he created was a type of meditation that involved the uprooting of all delusion in the mind and body.

You can right now depersonalise your experience of life by switching from this mistaken sense of a small 'I' to a larger sense: you are a god experiencing a simulator called 'another random life on earth'.

Get in the habit of recognising that life is just 'like this'. Relationships too are just 'like this'. There's no good or bad, and there's certainly no perfection. Every time something hurts, every time someone annoys you, every time you find yourself crushed by yet another disappointment, stop a second and think, *OK, all right, I'm experiencing life as a little, tender human, and it's supposed to be 'like this'.*

You were born for this. You chose this. And you will grow from this.

Don't be afraid to love. You invented love. It pours out of you as though you were a New York City fire hydrant in a disaster movie.

Just get out of its way.

THE FEAR MATRIX

If you're feeling low while you're reading this, pay really close attention to your actions. Are you still feeding yourself now and again? Are you still cleaning your teeth, washing your body, making efforts to work and stay connected to people even though it requires so much energy? Are you still charging your laptop for another series, refilling the kettle for a second brew of the same Pukka tea bag? That's love.

When you're faced with overwhelming fear the only solution is to lean into love. It's something I noticed the first time I proposed to someone. I was a little older than 30 and battling depression. My mind was full of so many confusing emotions and thoughts and negativity, but in the background, quiet as a mouse, there was still love.

We were in a forest in Brazil. She'd just discovered that her family were bankrupt, and her father was depressed. My girlfriend was also depressed. So was all Brazil, actually. People were out on the streets protesting. In Brazil at that time, there was fear everywhere, so we turned to love. The morning I proposed, I kissed her and told her that when she opened her eyes again, everything, absolutely everything would be better. She opened her eyes, and I had a ring in my hand. It was her grandmother's. Her father, who hadn't had the will to leave his armchair, had found the energy to search the cellar and give it to me. Love saved the day. That night we danced on the streets of São Paulo in the middle of a protest with half a million people. All of us imagined that we were part of a revolution, that together, singing, holding hands on streets that ordinarily wouldn't be safe to walk on, we could change the world.

Months later, she and I would break up, and Brazil would fall into an even worse economic state with even greater inequality – yet briefly, very briefly, we managed to stem the tide of fear.

The same thing happened when my dad was brought to an intensive care unit a few years back. The space was lit up like a moon landing. His body was punctured with tubes and syringes. My father was on a hero's dose of morphine. Day and night. His hands were cold to the touch. My father has come closer to death more times than a gravedigger, yet I've never seen him as frightened as in those days in the ICU.

I asked people to meditate for him. My mother got her church group to pray for him. If there was a machine for measuring attention, my dad, lying in his Velcro-sealed gown in a hospital bed, would have been off the charts. Each prayer, each positive intention, each time he defied the multiple predictions and flirted with the nurses was an act of love and a finger in the face of fear.

The first time I taught a meditation class was to a group of men who had just been released from a prison in Limerick. I was scared again. Not that they'd hurt me, just that they wouldn't listen to me. That I would be found out as an imposter. I sat in the car outside the draughty building where we met, and as the rain beat down on the windscreen, I repeated the phrase, *you are love, you are love, you are love.*

I'll fess up. I was whispering over a scream. *You are love, you are love* was barely audible beneath the roar of *You are a fraud, you are a fraud.*

Repeat after me: you are love, you are love, you are love.

If you try hard enough, eventually you will feel it. Keep faking it until you make it.

Fear keeps us small

See, this is the thing: fear cannot exist where there is love. When you are frightened, wrap yourself up in love.

The material world is not as solid as it seems. Science knows. Meditators know. The world of the meditator is more like a concept. It's vivid, it's enticing, but it's not real. It's empty. Now, you won't catch me walking out in front of a bus or jumping off tall buildings – the emptiness still hurts. But it does help to make sense of our fear.

No animal on this planet is born quite as helpless as you or me. A giraffe is up and walking within 15 minutes of being born. We're born with such great need. Babies cry because it's all so overwhelming, so frightening. The fear we experience in early childhood plays out in every action of our adult lives. It explains why we have the systems we do, why our attachments are so fraught with insecurity, why we only exist through the validation of others, why we impose conditions on our love like *Till death us do part.*

Fear is what keeps us small. It's what wakes us up in the middle of the night to go downstairs and open a laptop that isn't ours and read the emails.

I had a girlfriend who used to read my messages on my phone. It was a Samsung flip phone that never had any credit. Simple times. I think I got messages from about five people. *C u l8r m8? Call me. Sup?* None of them were secret lovers. I found out.

'Why do you do it?'

'Because I'm jealous.'

'Why are you jealous? You see me every day, you know where I am every night.'

'Because I love you.'

All the drama we experience in relationships comes from our fear of losing love. That fear can be traced all the way to our birth, to those days when we were so dependent on someone else.

What are you afraid of?

The thing to understand is that fear is not something to shake off, it's something to explore. Fear is, as Pema Chodron writes, 'a sign that we are moving closer to the truth'.

The most loving thing you can do for yourself is to get to know the things you are afraid of.

My spiritual journey began when I was 34 years of age and I took part in an ayahuasca ceremony. I suppose the wise people up in the clouds would say my spiritual journey had begun many years previously, but, for me at least, it felt like everything pre-ayahuasca had been sitting around waiting for my number to be called out. If I'd still been with my fiancée, I might not have done it. But freshly single, we do new things.

Ayahuasca is such a profound psychedelic because it takes you on a tour of all your fears. It activates the amygdala of your brain and creates a type of PowerPoint presentation of everything you've experienced but wished you hadn't. Folks refer to it as a lifetime of therapy in a few hours.

I found myself back in the womb. I could feel my mother's fears all around me. I thought about death. I was on my back in the apartment of a friend's but in my mind, I was in utero surrounded by death. It was terrifying.

When I came round, I felt very different. I came home to my sad little apartment and cried for a few days, and then I signed up for my first meditation retreat.

Signing yourself up for uncomfortable, frightening but hugely beneficial experiences is love.

The first 34 years of my life were motivated by fear. The last seven have been motivated by fear as well, but also love.

Go tell Oprah

When I was a boy growing up, we used to mock each other if we shared too much. If one of the lads said something about a break-up, the standard reply wasn't 'Tell me more' or 'We're here for you', it was 'Go tell Oprah'.

For most of my life, whenever I felt vulnerability in my throat, I'd shut it down with 'Go tell Oprah'.

So I want to hand the rest of this chapter over to her. A mid-book healing ceremony for everyone who's ever swallowed their vulnerability. Burn your palo santo if you've got it.

> If we deny love that is given to us, if we refuse to give love because we fear pain or loss, then our lives will be empty, our pain will be greater.

Fear is a program that keeps us in a waking nightmare.
Love can wake us up.

Let's try.

WAKING UP FROM
THE DREAM

'A rat in a maze is free to go anywhere
so long as it's in the maze.'
—Margaret Atwood

We have much less free will than we think we have. Once you begin to examine your life, you'll discover that you do things because your parents did, because your friends do, because society expects it of you, because advertisers are suggesting it every time you pick up your phone.

I moved in with a partner not because I really wanted to, but because after a year or so of dating, it felt like the thing to do. I always broke up with any partner who lied to me, not because I was that upset by the lie but because it felt like the thing to do.

I've had friends come to me looking for advice and responded in a way that suggests there's no real freedom at all – *Well, buddy, it's the thing to do.*

The thing to do is what's keeping you asleep.

Waking up means recognising that the thing to do may not be the thing you necessarily want to do. Waking up means directing this laser-focused awareness to every single decision you make and basing your decisions not on the thing you should do but the thing you actually want to do.

What would Buddha do?

This is what Buddha did.

He determined that the human dilemma is this: nothing lasts, and the mistaken belief that things will last causes our lives to be miserable. This is the dream that we all find ourselves lost in, the dream of permanence, the dream woven by our thoughts.

Buddha set this all out in a four-step plan called the Four Noble Truths.

1. Life is unsatisfactory.
2. The lack of satisfaction comes from wanting things to be otherwise.

3. The end of dissatisfaction comes with the acceptance of things.
4. There is a path you can follow.

The path Buddha mentioned was a thing called the Eightfold Path. It describes how a person might live well, and therefore not suffer anymore. Its essence is this: focus on the reality as it is, not as you'd want it to be.

Don't get addicted

Our thoughts are totally in on this dream. They are a product of the environments we've been exposed to. They flash in front of us like pop-up ads all day, and especially at night. If you're wondering why you're addicted to TV series and social media, it's because they're designed to be addictive; but you are also designed to become an addict. Our thoughts ensure this – and we're addicted to them, too.

An addiction is any behaviour that has a short-term payoff and long-term negative consequences. I wrote that sentence as I poured my second cup of coffee of the morning. A coffee I don't really need that'll make me jittery in about 15 minutes, and unable to finish this chapter.

When it comes to love, many of us are addicts. We're addicted to finding love outside ourselves. We feel incomplete when we're alone. Society doesn't help. There's a war on single people. Single people can't afford homes. They pay more tax. They are bullied by advertising campaigns depicting happiness in a couple in the same way gamblers are bullied by campaigns showing people winning.

The reality as it is: Love is an inside job, and gambling algorithms want you to lose.

Wake up, sleepyhead

Buddha's solution to the problem of an unsatisfactory life was to observe rather than react to it. Watch your thoughts, watch your feelings, watch yourself. Imagine you're playing a top-down game where your character goes to work, meets people, has good days, has bad days, has dreams, has fears – but just observe it, don't get sucked in.

Be an expert on you, less the world you walk out into when you open your eyes in the morning.

Life and all its contents are a dream. Waking up means recognising the dream and knowing that the greatest relationship you will ever experience is the one where you trust, nourish and love yourself.

Waking up is subtle.

It involves going against the complicated programming inside you. I have caretaking programming. If someone doesn't need me, I don't feel safe around them. Of course I ended up doing what I do. All teachers are this way. They need the students just as much as the students need them. My way of waking up from this dream has been to try to enjoy relationships and friendships without needing to offer help.

Waking up from your programming means observing how you're acting and then rebelling against it.

We are all programmed to not love ourselves. You don't need me to tell you that. You can feel it every time you try to put yourself out there, when you pass a mirror, when you begin to speak in a group and all eyes turn towards you. Your programming is thick with guilt, shame, obligation and judgement. How many relationship decisions do you make based on what other people think?

This is not authentic love.

The *third* time I got engaged (please don't despair of me, readers) I no longer wanted to be with the person. We were clearly not a good match, but when she proposed to me, a part of my programming kicked in. The people-pleasing program. The side of me that couldn't say no. I wonder how many people are married because they couldn't say no? Because they can't rebel against their programming.

Buddha was a rebel. He led a rebellion against himself. His rebellion was becoming aware that he was dreaming.

What do you want?

One of the scariest things that happens when you wake up from a lifetime of being told what you should want is that briefly, you won't know what you want at all. You're lost, without a purpose, momentarily suspended in time, terrifyingly unclear about your desire, like a tourist at an all-day breakfast buffet in Las Vegas.

'There is great happiness in not wanting anything,' says the Indian teacher Jiddu Krishnamurti.

And he's right. There is so much joy in the rare feeling of being complete, content, full. We don't encounter this often, yet somehow we're always looking for it. I worked for a few years as a TV actor in Germany. I did beer commercials, barbecue commercials, car commercials. The one shot the directors always cared about was the 'look of contentment' shot.

You've drunk the beer, you've cooked the meat, you've parked the car, now turn to the camera, gaze into the distance and smile like you want nothing more in the world.

Wake up and love your body as it is. Love your mind as it is. Love your life as it is, in all its shambolic, underpaid glory.

'Again, Conor, but this time with even more contentment. *Uber*-contentment.'

It wasn't easy. I can remember one shoot, on a beach in
Barcelona, staring into the sun, make-up running into my
eyes, trying again and again, for over two hours, to perfect
the face of an Audi owner who wanted nothing more in
the world.

When I wake up in the morning, I resist the first thoughts
that are gathering, the initial prods of activity, urgency and
panic, and I try to just lie there with my body, bladder full,
head swimming, belly hungry, exploring my capacity to try
to be OK with not satisfying my wanting mind.

It doesn't always work, but when it does, this minor
rebellion makes me feel very powerful.

Our thoughts are designed to leave us feeling powerless.

Ignoring them will, over time, make you feel powerful
in ways you could never have imagined.

Set your intention

It is beautiful to not want, but when it comes to relationships – the thing we invest most of our emotional energy
in – it's good to have at the very least an idea. In the world
of spirituality, we call the spark of an idea an 'intention'.

Discipline is great. Energy is superb. But intention is key. If your intention is in the wrong place, then all this effort will just take you far in the wrong direction.

If your intention is to make money, you can make money, but you might not feel rich.

If your intention is to impress, then you might impress a whole bunch of people but not feel valued.

If your intention is to be loved, then you'll get bombarded with it from the outside but never nourish it on the inside.

How are your intentions around love?

Do you truly want it, or do you actually just want an unbroken chain of identikit lovers who leave no lasting impression apart from some pretty decent ambient playlists on Spotify?

In my early twenties I had a thing for partners who were leaving town. I somehow attracted people who were two or three months from going away. It happened twice, and each time I had just enough time to fall for them, but not so much that it ever went anywhere.

I'd say to friends, 'I don't know what's up with my luck. Why can't I just meet someone who lives here?'

Then in my late twenties I had a thing for partners who had drinking problems. I'd say to myself, *Why can't I just meet someone functional who responds to my calls, who takes care of their health, who doesn't fall asleep in her dinner?* Sigh.

All I want is love, I'd whisper into my pillow.

Are you sure? my pillow replied. *I mean I'm just a pillow, what do I know? But if you say you want love, and yet you keep on bringing these people home who are incapable of giving you love, maybe you need to check your intention. Romantic attraction is not the roll of a dice, it's a matter of intention.*

Thank you, pillow. Can I help you with anything?

A bit of fabric softener in the drum next time?

You got it.

If you are attracting the wrong thing into your life, check your intention. It's probably off.

I have spent the vast majority of my dating career thinking it was all about them. The reality was I didn't want the challenge that came with a mature, stable relationship, so I preferred to just keep dating addicts, avoidants and amazing people who were about to move 5,000 miles away.

Folks, it's never about them. It's always about us.

My neighbour dates musicians. Guitarists, drummers, dudes covered in tattoos who come home smoky and sleep all day. She constantly complains about them. They're not reliable. They can't be trusted. They leave skid marks in her toilet bowl.

'Have you ever tried dating a guy with a regular job and good bathroom etiquette?'

'Oh no way, a guy like that would think I'm a freak.'

It's up to you

What you want is related directly to what you think you deserve. If you keep on attracting people into your life who end up not being what you want, then you need to get your intention checked. This is how:

Make a list of everything you want in a partner.

Start saying no to everything that doesn't match up with that list. It's hard, I know. Winter is long. Being alone can be gruelling. Taking what comes to you can seem like the only way to survive. But if you really want a loving relationship where you will grow and not just experience the same frustrations over and over again, then you have to get out of your habit of attracting what you don't want.

Become that list yourself. If you want someone who loves their parents, love your parents. If you want someone who is healthy, get healthy. If you want someone who is open to therapy, best get you off to a therapist first.

Gandhi said, 'As a man changes his own nature, so does the attitude of the world change towards him.'

If your nature is brimming with value, self-worth and boundless love, then this will be the intention that you send out into the world.

You're in a restaurant. The menu is huge. It's like one of those Chinese places where the numbers run up into the hundreds. The waiter's hovering over you. This is maybe the fifth time he's come back to the table. He's patient. He won't judge, but he will only bring you what you order.

So what is it that you really want?

ARE YOU READY
FOR REAL LOVE?

If you're learning a foreign language, you'll come across a term called 'false friends'. False friends are two words in different languages that sound alike but have different meanings.

A magazine in English is not a *magasin* in French. Embarrassed in English is how you feel when you make a boo-boo, but *embarazada* in Spanish is when you make a baby. Romance is beautiful in English, but in Italian *romanzo* is just a novel. Any novel. Maybe not even a good novel.

I've taught languages before. Teaching false friends is always interesting, because even when the student learns that it makes no sense to use a false friend, they still want to use the term. Their brain is drawn to the familiarity. We're all drawn to the familiarity. Familiarity is just habit. Habit is just rhythm. It's the tune that gets stuck in your ear. I spent a month of my life with that 'Havana, ooh na-na, half of my heart is in Havana' song stuck between my ears. It drove me crazy, and because I sang it aloud, it drove everyone around me crazy too.

In the world of intimate relationships, love and attachment are false friends. We get them mixed up all the time, and they stick in our heads like an unwanted song, driving everyone crazy and ensuring our relationships fall to pieces.

Here are the Cliffs Notes:

Love is giving; attachment is taking

This is far from clear, though. You need to be very aware of what you're doing when you believe that you're being loving. You've got to forensically examine what's going on inside you. Often when we say we're acting out of love, we're really acting out of need.

If you're feeling insecure in your relationships, if you're exerting control over someone, if you experience jealousy when they meet new people or success comes their way, this is attachment, it's not love. I had a girlfriend who became very successful. It was kind of overnight. She was working as a fashion designer when suddenly she flew into the spotlight. *Vogue* wanted to take her picture. Every day she got emails and phone calls with new offers and opportunities, and every day my outside response was, 'That's so awesome', but inside I was thinking, *Much more of this success and she's going to leave me.*

I never said this, of course, but she could feel it all the same. We feel all the unsaid things.

'But I love you,' I'd say, when she'd suggest that maybe I resented some of her good fortune. That was a false friend. If I'd known better, and really, I don't say this just in order to excuse myself, but it is all simply about knowing better, I'd have said, 'You're right, I don't love you – I am attached to you. I need you. I want to hold on to you even if that means holding you back, and your success, your growth, it scares me.'

Love builds; attachment destroys

Real love is generous and giving. You can feel it as an energy inside you. It invigorates. It's fearless. It's boundless. It's limitless.

Attachment feels like you're in a fight. A fight that you might lose. You're never at ease.

Attachment keeps you up all night; love makes you sleep like a puppy.

Many of us are trained that to think that love is attachment. It's what we grew up with. Our parents grew up in systems of deep co-dependency. This is why love, for many of us, is something painful. This is not our fault. It's just familiar. If you go back to the Latin meaning of familiar, *famulus,* the translation means 'servant'. We are servants to the familiar. It controls us. It's the master. But its control is only an illusion. So much of what we believe to be true is an illusion.

Joseph Goldstein, the great meditation teacher, says this:

> One of the great misconceptions we often carry throughout our lives is that our perceptions of ourselves and the world are basically accurate and true, that they reflect some stable, ultimate reality. This misconception leads to tremendous suffering, both globally and in our personal life situations.

Our perception of love, much like our perception of ourselves, is not accurate. This is why we have attachments.

Love says: I want you to be happy.

Attachment says: I want you to make me happy.

It's a simple linguistic misunderstanding. A false friend of the heart. Attachment stunts your growth. We came here

Part 3
You

BE HERE NOW

Do you enjoy your own company?

Can you go for a walk on your own? Or take a holiday by yourself? Can you fall asleep at night? Can you listen? How about books? Do you manage to get to the end now and then? What about boredom – can you indulge it? What happens inside you when people are late, or when they flake?

Can you put your mind to a task and keep it in place until that task is done? Can you fritter away an afternoon lost in the slow creep of time? Can you put your mind to just staring out the window, and not react to the volley of aggressive insults you throw at your unproductive self?

You can be supremely content by simply bringing your attention to the present. I sneered at this idea once. I had spent so much time bringing my attention to work and relationships and my own ambition that it would have been far too painful to admit that I was wrong. You can grow addicted to the struggle too.

I heard an Eckhart Tolle interview where he was asked about his hobbies. In this interview, Eckhart Tolle replied that one of his favourite things to do is to simply stare out the window. When he said this, I knew that old ET was not only legit but, in all probability, a higher life form.

If you don't believe me, try it yourself.

*Look out the window. Sit back, relax.
See how long you can hold your
attention on this activity.*

Were you able to hold your attention on the scene outside your window for even just a few minutes? If you try doing this, you'll notice that you almost immediately come under attack from tiny impulses. Your bladder might tell you to go and pee. Your belly might tell you to go and eat. Your stress might tell you to go back to your computer, and the phone – or 'fresh horrors device', to quote Jenny Odell – in your pocket might tell you to pick it up to see what fresh horror awaits you. You will be bombarded by voices reminding you of tasks that you haven't done, and more often than not you'll give them your attention. But once you give something your attention, once you enter that stream, it's got you.

Your attention is the most valuable thing you possess. If consciousness is a type of mysterious essence that inhabits objects, and if our heads are full of largely negative thoughts, and our bodies are primed with biological urges that may not bring us lasting well-being (getting wildly turned on by an ex who we are trying very hard to build a boundary with, right?), then attention, more than anything else, is the most honest method we have for negotiating life.

We become what we pay attention to

I grew up in a deeply loving, chaotic, romantic and frightening home, where I had fun and love and precious little security. Naturally, it absorbed all my attention. Almost all of my relationships throughout my twenties were the same combination of loving and frightening. I had become what I'd paid attention to. We all do this. Our imagination is sourced from outside ourselves through the agenda-free lens of your attention.

Attention is pure and unbiased, and it's brutally honest.

If you spend an hour on Facebook, you will feel braindead.

If you only listen to the negative voices in your head, your experience of life will be negative.

If you are a hypochondriac, the anxiety you create eventually makes you ill.

If you consume a lot of news, you'll encounter a scary world full of fresh horrors.

If you consistently follow the same impulses, then you'll always be repeating the same lesson.

Cause and effect. What you pay attention to you become.

Stop the world, I want to get off

I have friends who live off-grid. It's not so hard to do any more. Back in the day, it was something that weirdos did, but perhaps there are more weirdos now, or it's simply become less weird to not want to participate so much in prescribed ways of living. Anyway, it's not so strange for people to grow their own food and create their own energy any more. In the future, it'll probably be what we all do. My friends who live off-grid have their own problems, but as most of them pay no attention to the news, they don't share our global problems. Their attention is fixed on what's coming up through the soil, or how their rescue dogs are rehabilitating, or the magical fermentation process transforming jars of cucumbers into jars of pickles above the kitchen sink.

Often, they're silent. They are in tune with the weather. They are radically simple people. I watch them with the same wonder that I watch the pigeons picking through the leftover oatmeal on my balcony.

These friends pay attention to a very different world than I do, a more peaceful, more tangible world. They don't worry about Amazon colonising space, they worry about the coming rain, and because of this it's a joy to be in their company. I often walk in on them to find them sitting and staring out the window. At this, they're masters.

The ability to be present like this, to simply stare out a window, our attention fixed, under control, is a type of superpower. There are some days I can do it. But almost all the time when I try, I'll feel a force rise up and drag me to the kitchen to prep soup, or towards the laptop to buy things I really don't need.

I know I'm not alone in this.

We are more alone than ever

When I was on dating apps, they would send me alerts on a Sunday evening: *there's a swipe surge in your area.* In the modern world, Sunday evening is the evening when most of us are alone, the evening when most single people find themselves staring out the window. Instead of a surge, they could call it our collective inability to be present with just ourselves at the toughest time of the week. Sunday evening is the most painful part of the week. We can accept that weekdays are shit, because we've been accepting that since we were schoolkids, but if the weekend's also shit, then what's the point?

We are more alone now than we've ever been. For social animals, this is tough. Our response to tough times is to disassociate. As children we do this at the dinner table, when we pretend we can't hear our parents, and as adults we do it on our phones when we pretend not to hear our partners.

I like to talk on the phone. I want to hear your voice, understand the nuances, the breath, the mispronunciations, the background noises as you walk your dog. Messaging, to me, often feels like a way of being there but not really there. I suspect that the more we message the less we really want to communicate. As with tennis, we're just trying to get the ball back into the other half of the court.

Our phones are the most wonderful devices imaginable. I teach on my phone. I get taught on my phone. My phone has led me to tiny Buddhist centres in new cities for drop-in meditations, and off-the-beaten-track Vietnamese restaurants for pho. My phone can tell me what bird I've just shared my lunch break with in the park.

I love my phone, but, Christ, I've never known anything that can create as many opportunities for me to not engage with the present. If I'm lonely, it sucks me right in. Staring out the window, then, being present with nothing, is a radical way of just being with the reality of your loneliness, the presence of loneliness.

When Pema Chodron is asked why she meditates she answers: to become more flexible and tolerant to the present moment. How tolerant are you to the present moment? If we had tiny electronic tickers that ran around our foreheads in bright neon lights and alerted people to what was really going on with us, most of the time those tickers would say something like 'I can't handle the present right now, please leave me alone'.

So much of our spiritual and relationship paths are predicated on our capacity to be present, to resist the constant barrage of information inside and outside ourselves and just be with what is in the moment. And when we can be in the moment, when we can just stare out the window, we get to see that the world isn't something that appears, but rather something that reflects.

'We but mirror the world,' said Gandhi.

It sounds inspiring, but ultimately kind of elusive, kind of vapid, right? Many of these expressions sound unreal: Feel your feelings. Be true to yourself. Love everyone. They remain intangible until you live them, embody them.

How might that work?

If you want to feel rich, be generous.

If you want to feel good, give someone else praise.

If you want to feel less lonely, find someone in need.

If you want to feel satisfied, practise wanting what you already have.

If you want to stop feeling unlucky, imagine that you're choosing everything that's happening to you.

If you want to grow, do something you've never done before.

If you want to know who you are, remove all your distractions.

If you want to feel love, love somebody else.

When you can begin to cherish your attention and embody the present, the world becomes invested with other layers of understanding, and wisdom.

Wisdom in Buddhism is called paññā. Paññā means paying attention to the supramundane. Tapping into what exists beyond your everyday problems. It means going beyond the limits of your apparent human existence. I say apparent because, come on, we know there's something more to us, right?

Pay attention to what bugs you

A good friend of mine has a friend who is unpredictable. He is often rude to waiters. He gets angry when things are late. His dog is also unpredictable. When they go to the park together the dog will sometimes jump on people, who then get upset.

'Why would anyone go to the park if they're going to be upset by a dog?' he shouts.

This guy is unreasonable. My friend complains about him. He doesn't know what to do. We talk about the situation a little longer. He knows that he won't just drop his friend, but he doesn't know how to deal with his unpredictability. He describes him a little more. 'He's a good person, I can see the good in him, he's just a little lost and messy.'

'It sounds like you're describing yourself from a couple of years ago.'

'That's exactly who I'm describing,' he admits. 'He's me.'

Everyone we meet is a reflection of our own relationship to ourselves.

When we can be very present with the things that annoy us, we'll see that our annoyance rarely has anything really to do with them, and that they are actually a valuable source of learning.

One of the greatest acts of love towards ourselves is to commit to being present with our experience of life.

Show up in your own life

At one time in my life, I really thought I was monastery-bound. I mean, I did check myself into the monastery, but I didn't imagine that I'd leave again after a month. As I became more present in the monastery, I realised that I hadn't been so present with my life before. I'd missed things: the smile on my mother's face when I arrived in the door, the smell of toast that somebody else is making for you, the wedge of bodies on a commuter train, the small talk with someone who's asked you for change, the awkwardness of eye contact in a lift, the weird dances in restaurants when we realise we're in the path of a waiter carrying four plates. I wanted to go back again.

Agnes Martin is my favourite artist. I think I was initially drawn to her because I'd read that she lived way out in the desert. She was radically removed, and this was something I'd aspired to. But then she said this:

> A lot of people withdraw from society, as an experiment.
> So I thought I would withdraw and see how enlightening
> it would be. But I found out that it's not enlightening.
> I think that what you're supposed to do is stay in the
> midst of life.

The way to stay in the midst is to stay present. The way to stay in a relationship – with yourself and with other people – is to stay present.

If you want to be good at staying present, carve out a little time to practise staring out the window.

YOUR PAIN

'The essence of trauma is disconnection from ourselves. Trauma is not terrible things that happen from the other side – those are traumatic. But the trauma is that very separation from the body and emotions.' — Gabor Maté

'If you don't like feeling lonely, don't get married.' A married bartender said that to me on our first shift together in a bar on Long Island. At the time I was just at the beginning of a relationship. That morning I'd been late to pick her up from the bus station and all day she'd been giving me the silent treatment.

I felt rejected by her. She felt abandoned by me. If we'd been wiser young souls, we might have understood that what was happening to us wasn't vindictive, it was just our learned responses to circumstances beyond our control. But we weren't wise, and we broke up soon afterwards.

Meet the runaway bride

My automatic response in relationships is flight. I have a friend who calls me the runaway bride. Closeness scares me because I find it hard to trust. Moments in relationships where I'm forced to rely on a partner – navigating in traffic, when I'm ill, when I'm not able to do everything myself – can shake me to the core. One forgotten message is enough to send me into a spiral of suspicion.

Trust is to love what wheels are to racing cars. So much of the love I've experienced in this life has been a love with no wheels, a chassis scraping along the road at low speed, sparks flying, deafening noise, bystanders looking on in anticipation of the impending disaster.

Sigh!

'Be kind, for everyone you meet is fighting a battle you know nothing about,' said Ian Maclaren. We are all coping as best we can with whatever pain we've been dealt. Love is our commitment to understanding our pain and our discipline to heal it.

My friend who called me the runaway bride is also an astrologer. She looked at my chart and informed me that I had Chiron in the twelfth house. 'What's Chiron?', I asked. 'It's the wounded healer,' she said. When I heard this, I identified strongly with it. I felt vindicated. *My life's been hard,* I told myself, *and now the stars have confirmed it.* I am a wounded healer. This excuses all my bad behaviour. I'm different, marked, a victim of circumstances beyond my control. Shortly afterwards I discovered we all have Chiron in our charts. We're all, astrologically at least, wounded healers. No exceptions.

Your pain is the handicap life gives you during this particular race. Your commitment and discipline to heal this pain is where you flex your capacity to love.

The crack is where the light gets in, right?

Pain is an energy that becomes trapped in our bodies. Energy wants to move. Your pain doesn't want to stay in your body. Our pain appears when our essential needs are not met. What matters is not so much what happens, but how you feel about what happens. What happened to you can never be changed. The horrible, unfair treatment you received is etched in stone, but you are not etched in stone. You are an organic flow of experiences. Your cells replicate. Every seven to ten years you are made anew. The traumatic events that have happened in your life can never be erased, but the pain can be. The pain is the story you tell yourself about the event. Oftentimes that story is that you deserved it, that you brought it on yourself, that you are unlovable or that this is how things always will be.

Work through it, not around it

My parents were deeply loving but suffered from addiction and poverty. Growing up in their care I didn't get what I needed. That was traumatic. We take this trauma into relationships. It erupts in triggering, icy silences, acting out, anger, running away, confusion, so much confusion, so much hurt.

In almost every single relationship I've been in since I left that home, I have not got what I needed. My partners have been either addicts, immature or selfish. That's my trauma. It's the story that I need to take care of people, that I can't upset a partner and that bad behaviour in a relationship is probably my fault.

The last time I was engaged was back at the beginning of my meditation path. My partner at the time was a very loving, very kind workaholic. She was always stressed out. Her body would come alive in rashes after she opened her emails. My role in the relationship was to take care of her. This meant often supressing my needs. Even to medi-tate. Meditation triggered her, because she felt abandoned whenever I'd sit in silence. You're doing it again, she'd say when she found me sitting on the floor with my eyes closed.

Rather than work through it, we worked around it.

I meditated in secret, in my car, outside on park benches, sometimes at friends' places.

'Where were you?'

'Oh, nowhere,' I'd say.

'Don't lie to me, you were meditating again. It's written all over your face!'

We never quite managed to heal our pain in that rela-tionship, but we got to know it very well. It wrapped itself around us until one morning, living apart as an experiment in rebuilding our love, she texted me to say she couldn't go on any more.

Love is a commitment to healing your pain and cre-ating space for other people to heal theirs. For as long as that's possible.

Your past doesn't define you

Relationships are important, because they are the places where we are once again exposed to the same pain we had as children. Relationships are like a UV light across a hotel mattress – all the stains appear. Only this time we're grown-ups and we can process it, we can self-soothe, re-parent and heal. Whatever happened to you can never unhappen to you, but how it made you feel about yourself is just a story.

To be in a relationship, we need to get better at understanding our pain, our partner's pain and our collective pain. We live in a heavily polluted world, separated from nature, separated from genuine love and wedded to systems of relationship, governance and work habits that are not designed with our well-being or expansion in mind. We are a traumatised people on a traumatised planet. We need to take our pain seriously. We need to create spaces for our pain to be released.

For some it's natural spaces; for others it's dance floors. A friend of mine in Berlin goes to clubs where she can safely dance topless, and in this way reclaim her relationship with her body. Each night out, drenched in sweat and glitter, she is slowly returning back to the good feelings she originally had about her own skin.

Another friend bought a van and travels the south of Europe alone with a huge support network of friends and van-lifers. It's her way of sticking a finger up at a childhood of restrictions and cruelty. It's her way of celebrating freedom. She watches the sun rise and set each day. They are her only 'have tos'.

to grow, and occasionally get songs stuck in our heads, but mostly to grow. Learning to love in a way that gives rather than takes is a hard lesson to learn, but if you can make it stick, all your relationships, including the one with yourself, will blossom.

You are love. You come from love.
You are worthy of love.

If you were to commit yourself to healing your pain right now, what might that commitment involve? A van, a dance floor, a relationship where you are seen, heard, loved and respected?

Life is both our poison and our medicine. Learn about your pain. Watch how it shapes your life, and even at times governs your life. We don't have to allow it to define our lives and our possibilities. Transformation is not only possible, it's inevitable. I say this from the point of view of a person who believes in reincarnation. YOLO for me is You Only Live One thousand times. If I don't get to the bottom of it this time, I'll just have to deal with it the next time, right?

The most loving thing you can do in this life is to take your pain, and our collective pain, seriously.

Transformation is not only possible, it is inevitable.

Your purpose is acceptance

High spirituality, non-secular Buddhism, some witches, and the type of people you meet at festivals who like to juggle glass balls and eye-gaze will tell you that you choose your own life. The world and your unique experience in it are a ride at some cosmic fairground that you lined up for, paid for and opted in to.

Complain all you like, but you did read the 900,000-page document before you signed the terms and conditions, no? Not only is everything going to plan, it's going to your plan. The god, the divine shift supervisor behind all this, may not be some white-haired uber-parent in the sky, but actually yourself.

Life, this life, is a meal that you made for yourself.

There is no hard proof of this, of course. It's unsubstantiated. So much in life is up for grabs like this: consciousness is a mystery, death is a mystery, the human appendix is a mystery. But there are clues in the shadows and lessons in the mysteries. Just because we can't explain something fully doesn't mean we can't engage with it. I don't know why many meditation practices work; all I know is that meditation has transformed my life and the lives of the people I meditate with.

We grow through pain

The purpose of life is much like the purpose of massage.

Every now and again I go to a lady for a Thai massage. Her name is Thini, and she comes from Chiang Mai. Now my body is tight like a bike chain. On cold days, I'm more timber than flesh. I blame it on growing up in a damp house. I have bursts of yoga discipline, but then weeks where my mat gathers dust and cobwebs.

My workaround is to go to this lady for a massage every so often. Thini is incredibly strong. I don't know, because we have no common language, but my belief is that she was a wrestler long before she became a masseuse. For 60 minutes she bends and pummels my body until it's got no more resistance than soggy paper. The pain is immense. My face turns scarlet. Sometimes I cry.

Thini laughs. 'Good, good, good,' she says, the way a loved one might when removing a splinter from your hand.

There are moments in the session when I want to give up. There are times when I want to storm out of the place, but then I remember I wanted this, I paid for this, I volunteered for this, and I decided to do this, and my motivation was love for myself.

How are you doing today? Do you want to storm out of the place too? Have you got an impressively strong Thai lady on your back?

Your life is a gift you've given yourself. The gift is occasionally painful, often confusing and routinely devastating, but it is the most loving gift you could have given yourself, because ultimately this is what will make you grow.

We grow through pain. We grow through discomfort.

Knowing this, how could you have any doubts that the universe, that god, that you, or the celestial geeks – whoever you'd like to credit – pulling the levers up in the sky could be anything other than loving?

At the end of each massage I always hug Thini, and she smiles at me, and I smile back through puffy eyes. 'Good, good, good,' she says.

THE ONE

'There is nothing to cling to in this world.
Ask yourself, "What can I take with me
when I die?"' —Dipa Ma

Where I grew up, a rock was real because if you kicked it, your foot hurt. In the Brahmic tradition in India, for something to be real it has to be real all the time. It has to have being, and it has to shine by its own light. If an object is dependent upon another object to shine, then it's not real. Anything that takes its sense of existence from something else is not truly real. Do you see where I'm going with this?

If you only come alive when someone shines their light on you, are you ever really alive?

When I first started dating people, I believed that I would one day stumble upon a person who would, in one fell swoop, clear out my depression, my anxiety and the weird feelings that I had about my body: my slumpy shoulders, my chicken legs, my patchy stubble and my lack of any discernible bum when I wore jeans. I believed that there was such a person, maybe at work, maybe in the coffee shop or coming around the next corner, who would take one deep look at me, and in that moment all my insecurities would drop to the ground like beads of shimmering water from a hairy dog who's just taken a bath in a pothole.

Readers, I found her.

And then a while later, I found her again. And then, believe it or not, I found her again. Some time later I found her again. One time I found her online. I even found her, lost her and found her for a second time. Another time I found her and didn't even manage to speak to her, but it worked all the same. She looked at me, smiled, and all the negativity shook loose.

Over the course of a long time in serial monogamy, I became so good at finding the one, or at least 'a one', that I never really had to live with the negative feelings I had of myself. This is, unfortunately, not love, it's addiction. It's an exhausting cycle of highs and lows and precious little self-examination. If you're looking for someone to take the negative relationship you have with yourself away, you will find them. But just like weeds and facial herpes, when the negative feelings grow back, you'll have to treat them with something, or someone, new again.

This is not why you came to earth.

Finding the one, searching for the one and even believing that you've found the one aren't ways of healing, they're ways of avoiding. The whole point of any spiritual adventure – and when I say spiritual, I don't mean beads, hand tattoos and creepy eye-gazing, I mean exploring the mystery of you – is not to bypass but to experience fully. What we're trying to experience is this: You are the one you've been waiting for.

Byron Katie said that. I remember when I first read her quote, I puked in my mouth a little. It sounded so corny, so impractical, so tidy. This is something I've discovered. If you find beautiful, uplifting quotes about love and happiness corny, it's because you've been so badly wounded in this life that you won't even allow yourself to imagine that love and happiness are possible. I read many spiritual books with a little puke in my mouth. When they spoke about joy, or peace or the bliss that descends when you're not doing anything, I would put the book to one side and say, 'Cool, guys, you do you and I'll do me.'

Doing me meant holding out for someone special to come along, while casually avoiding my own role in my own life.

You can't buy self-love

Society teaches most of us that there is one person out there just for them. We use swans as an example. They mate for life, we say, forgetting that swans are by and large not neurotic, don't carry baggage and are almost never on social media, and as a result are probably much easier to satisfy. We look to our parents and, if their marriage was a train wreck, maybe our grandparents. We study the past for examples of how to be in the future, forgetting that we're a rapidly evolving cluster of molecules with no reverse gear.

We need new models, but mostly we need to give up on the idea of the one, because it's deeply unfair. It perpetuates a lie that there is something outside you that will make the gnawing feeling inside you go away.

We grew up under the conditioning of capitalism and the patriarchy, so we've learned that in order to be happy we have to learn how to survive and live as little worker ants.

*There is nothing outside of you that will
make the gnawing feeling go away.*

Surviving in this system has nothing to do with who you are and everything to do with how many nuts you've gathered. It's no wonder then that relationships are so difficult under this paradigm, because we approach them like consumers.

Capitalism will eventually end. We are, deep down, a compassionate people. It might not look that way when we spend time online, but in real life, we don't step over each other. In real life, eye contact counts. A system based on competition and cruelty doesn't suit us, and can't last. Unchecked inequality can't last.

But seeing as that's where we find ourselves today, we need to explore our relationship with relationships inside this system of values, profit, cost analysis and anti-love agendas.

Learn to value yourself

I like to think that I value myself, but when someone else comes along, someone who takes a casual interest in us, someone who we are trying to impress, we begin to value ourselves a whole lot more. This is something to be curious about.

If you are the one you've been waiting for, then you need to start working on being your best, not to attract someone else but to feel good about being you. Don't get me wrong, compliments make my heart flutter like the best of us, but have you ever sat very quietly, closed your eyes, brought your attention inward and, with a sincerity that would make a telenovela actor blush, said, 'I love you and I'm so damn proud of you.'

> *Sit quietly, close your eyes, bring your attention inward and say,*
> *'I love you and I'm so damn proud of you.'*

How was that? Did you skip it? As experiences go, proclaiming our undying love for ourselves can be as uncomfortable as taking our clothes off in front of a stranger. But it's a necessary experience, because the harder it is to do, the more likely you will be to try to find someone to do it for you. That's the consumer's approach to self-help. It's short-cuts and workarounds. A spiritual person (and if you've made it this far into the book, this means you) recognises that, when something is hard or painful, the wise response is to get very quiet and get very curious.

Don't try to solve your problems, just get curious about them.

Think about the feeling you get when someone says they love you. How just a few small words can make you feel complete. And now imagine that you could say them to yourself. Experiencing self-love, or even an attempt at self-love, can be awkward. You might want to run away from it.

I had a friend once who made me shout it across a valley. We had been hiking all day and I'd been telling him all about a relationship that had just collapsed. He's a good friend. He'd been listening to me talk in circles all morning. 'I don't know what happened, man, it's so painful to let her go. I don't know why.' It was so perfectly clear that we weren't a good match. The first night we met she was on a come-down from a session and I was on my way back from a sound bath meditation – I mean, how different could we be?

'You don't love yourself,' he said.

'Say what?'

'I've been listening to you make excuses all morning. Just be honest, you don't love yourself.'

'But I must. I eat healthy. I buy myself nice things. I'm a friggin' meditator.'

'That's not enough,' he said. 'If you really loved yourself, you'd never get into relationships with people just because they loved you back.'

'Maybe you're right,' I said.

It was then that he had the genius idea that I should shout 'I love myself!' from the top of the Glendalough valley. It was a Monday. Apart from some deer and sheep, we were the only people there. Cloud was obscuring the lakes below, and rain was coming down from the Spinc. I had bog water in my boots. I'm not sure I've ever set foot in Wicklow and not got bog water in my boots.

'If you loved another person, you'd do it. So why can't you proclaim it for yourself?'

'But I'll look like a complete tool. It's silly. It feels stupid for a grown man to shout, "I love myself".'

'I won't tell anyone.'

'I certainly won't tell anyone either,' I replied, and looked out over the clouds.

So that's out of the bag.

I shouted 'I love myself!', and he encouraged me to try again, only louder. So this time, I shouted 'I love you!', and then I started repeating it like it actually meant something. As awkward as it may sound, and as difficult as I found it, the more I said those three small words, the more I really believed them.

This is another good one: the sooner you become honest about something the sooner your suffering goes away.

This is how we learn to value ourselves.

Be honest with yourself

It's interesting. My last relationship was a doozy. We moved together from Europe to California after dating for less than half a year. When we landed in America our pace doubled. Inside a month, we went from jokingly booking hotels and guesthouses as a married couple to getting engaged. We drove out into the desert on a whim and met a realtor, who offered us a couple of acres of dirt and coyote tracks for next to nothing. One night, while we were waiting for paperwork to seal the deal, we went out to the land and built a campfire.

'We should get a contract drawn up before we buy the land,' she said.

'How come?'

'In case we break up. I don't want to get thrown out of my home like my mother.'

Neither of us had ever mentioned the word break-up in the relationship. In young, unstable, rapidly developing relationships you often don't. It's the drunk-in-love equivalent of saying the word Voldemort and alerting the Death Eaters to your location.

And, boy, did they ever come.

Something happened after that. Almost at the same time, both of us pulled back. It was as though the subconscious part of us came to an arrangement, on that plot of land, that it was best to go our separate ways. But it never informed the conscious part of us. From there on out, we entered a kind of crocodile death-roll, picking fights over everything until every discussion ended with one of us saying 'I need space'.

It was funny. We lived in the desert. It was as close as possible to living off the earth while still being on earth. You could go out our front door and walk three miles in most directions and not bump into another person. There were times when I'd wander off for a pee and think, *If I tripped and couldn't get up again, nobody would find me here for a hundred years.* Still, out on the flat, empty plains of the Mojave, we couldn't get enough space from each other.

In those days, our style was kind of scruffy, because for the most part we were just wandering around in cold winds and sandstorms. Scarves and old jeans, military boots and beanies. But in our last weeks, I noticed she'd begun to wear dresses and put on make-up and spend a little longer on her hair. I commented on it once. I think I said something like, 'Is there someone else?'

But apart from a gas station and a few preppers hiding out behind rolls of razor wire and hand-painted 'Trespassers will be shot' signs, there was nobody else. I didn't know it then, but she was actually learning to value herself again. When we break up with people, we're often inspired to make an effort for ourselves again. We're inspired to fill the need for love we had all by ourselves.

Søren Kierkegaard said that 'life is not a problem to be solved, but a reality to be experienced'.

It's important to experience how hard it is for us to find value in ourselves when we're not being attracted by other people, but when we do realise this, the way out is to take responsibility for it. Taking responsibility means doing the work. Very simply, it means getting honest about your relationship with yourself, and then working on improving that.

Have confidence in yourself

You might have noticed that we're at a critical juncture in our species history. Truth is up for grabs. I grew up in the 1980s, when what you saw on the news was how the world was. Of course it wasn't always accurate, but we believed it all the same. Seeing was believing.

We're now moving into a period in our history where feeling is believing. Reality, something most of us could agree on, has become a matter for debate. Everything is real, but nothing, absolutely nothing, is literal. That's how you survive a reality that is presented to us in the form of a hologram. This world isn't bad, it's just not anything like what we think it is.

It's messy out there. And this tendency to look for other people to give us the answers is the same tendency that propels us out into the world looking for love. It's a lack of confidence in ourselves.

People can listen to you talk about your relationship woes, they can give examples from their own experience, they can tell you what they would do, but nobody can tell you what to do. This is just a decision you have to come to on your own. Discovering that you are the one in charge means that you will finally learn to trust your own voice. Learning to trust your own voice is the most important thing any of us can do right now. Trust is how we get through the tough situations that we encounter.

You are exactly where you're meant to be right now. Whatever situation you find yourself in, whether it's a period of deep loneliness or sadness, or you've just lost someone or something, this is exactly what you need to be experiencing right now. We want sunshine, we want multiple orgasms, we want people saying, 'You are completely right, you're always completely right, how did you get so

good at being completely right 100 per cent of the time?'
But wherever you are, just experience it.

If you were the last person on earth you'd quickly discover something. You'd realise, as you walked around the
ruins of civilisations, that the most important relationship
was always just the one with yourself. After some days of
pottering around looking for phone reception, you'd stop
looking altogether. You'd begin to spend more time inside
exploring the mechanics of your own mind. You'd find a
home there. You'd stumble across a vast internal valley
enshrouded by clouds and mist and floating crystals (I'm
not promising anything).

You'd connect to the part of you that at this stage
understands that it's human but also weirdly divine, and
you'd shout, weakly at first, but slowly reaching a roar, 'I
love you, man, I love you, man, I love you!' Or, as Byron
Katie said, and we'll say it one more time, so you understand very clearly: You are the one you've been waiting for.

WHY IT'S SCARY TO LOVE YOURSELF

'Do not expect to receive the love from someone else you do not give to yourself ... The light of love is always in us, no matter how cold the flame. It is always present, waiting for the spark to ignite, waiting for the heart to awaken.' —bell hooks

Nobody tells you that you need to love yourself until you're in deep trouble. We don't even mention it until life has raked you over the coals, drained you of your youth, snuffed out the bright flame of your enthusiasm and left you with a considerable credit card debt. We don't tell people how important it is to love themselves until they're at rock bottom.

Only then, with fading energy, leaky self-esteem and enough negative thoughts to down an elephant, do we pass on this secret. We mention it as though it were as easy as moisturising a dry spot, as though it was something we'd mastered long ago ourselves. *Hey, I've been listening to you for a while now, and from what I see you simply need to love yourself.*

'You simply need to love yourself.' We wait to say these words until it's so late in the game, until the person is so broken, until if we don't say it, we might not ever get a chance to say it. I don't know why we leave it so late, or reserve this unique but difficult piece of advice for emergencies.

It's as if we're worried that if we tell a reasonably stable person to love themselves, they might turn into an egomaniacal monster. If you tell someone who's not lying flat on the floor halfway through a box of tissues to love themselves they'll turn into Narcissus, and then you'll be complicit in the trail of destruction their runaway regard for their own happiness inevitably causes.

I think we're afraid to love ourselves.

Don't wait for others to accept you

When I was 12, I started putting Brylcreem in my hair. I had red curls that pointed up towards the sky like columns of fire. Firenados crossing my scalp. Hair that looked like clumps of knotted grass on the wind-beaten scalp of a hillside. You saw me coming. It was a problem, but we all had the same problem where I grew up. We were raised on TV programmes starring heroes with straight blonde hair, yet we were a tribe of wild boys who looked like we got pretty in the morning by putting our fingers in sockets.

The first day I went to school with Brylcreem in my hair was also the last. 'Creighton loves himself,' people said. 'Who do you think you are, loving yourself?' It went on for an entire morning. At lunchtime I washed it out in the sink, but still, all the way up to last class, kids, even from the years below, emboldened by a sign of weakness in an older animal, would come up and mockingly ask, 'Do you love yourself?'

It's almost 30 years since those days at school, and although I've done enough work to know better, the desire to be accepted for who I am, and what grows of its own volition from my scalp, is still strong.

If we're honest about what we enjoy most about the early on-boarding stage of a new romance, it's the acceptance. If someone says something nice about my hair, I'm putty in their hands. And how good does it feel when someone says you're funny? Or when they listen, the whole way now, to the end of one of your stories, and reply with nods, enthusiasm and excitement? Or how about that curtain-call moment of potential mortification when you take your clothes off in front of them and they smile at the body that you can't even bring yourself to look at on some days?

When I first started writing articles for magazines, I'd wait until they also went online and then read, re-read and refresh the comments, soaking up any praise. Hook it to my veins. If the comments were negative, and they often were, it could send me into a downward spiral.

If you look at the areas of your life where other people's enthusiasm really matters, you'll begin to see a map of where you most need to do the work. This is the chink in your armour. Are you a secret poet embarrassed by your words? Are you ashamed of how your legs look in tight jeans? Do you have a suspicion that your stories are boring? Do you feel somehow unworthy? If you do, all it takes is for someone to sweep in and accept these parts of you, and you'll find yourself falling for them.

Self-love means developing a level of independence where you want the love of others but don't need it. Many of us come at this the wrong way round. When we realise

how much other people's love means to us, and how unstable that energy is, we shut the door completely, denying
ourselves both love from inside and love from outside. You
see this in some people – maybe you even see it in yourself
– and it's heart-breaking.

When I was about 26, I fell in love with a very sweet,
independent and strong woman who kindly invited me
to come to Vancouver with her. Perhaps if I'd been a little
more aware of the importance of self-love I wouldn't have
moved somewhere where I knew nobody and had no community, but when your tank is empty, you do things like
this. She was the life-size equivalent of a positive comment
beneath an article. Be careful when you notice that all your
eggs are in someone else's basket. Those eggs should really
be in yours.

After a few weeks in Vancouver she asked when I was
leaving, and I remember feeling so wounded by her words
that I didn't cry, I didn't even make a fuss, I just booked my
flight for the next morning and came home. At a conscious
level I marked that relationship off as a lesson learned, but
at a subconscious level, at the level of my programming, I
had already written new coding to ensure that this kind
of thing would never happen again. I had reprogrammed
myself to never attach properly again. Every relationship

I entered into after that was built upon one simple rule: I will let people come close, but I will never really let myself love them.

Love is as you believe it to be. If we believe love to be painful, or if we don't believe that it's possible, then nothing will change that.

Your programming is trying to help you by softening your experience of the world. It's like a parent who doesn't want to let their child out to play on the street because they might learn curse words and bad habits. But you and I both know that cursing and getting in trouble are two of the best things you can do as a kid, and so is learning to love with no fear of getting hurt.

Self-love is how we do this. It's our protective shield. Self-love is about generating so much love inside that when we go out into the world and people are enthusiastic about us, we don't fall weak at the knees or roll over on our backs, but we acknowledge it. Yes, my life is pretty good, I worked very hard making it this way.

Channel your inner four-year-old

Has anyone ever given you a compliment and, instead of blushing, or pushing it aside, you thought, *Yes, I know*? Children do this.

Wow, you're really good at drawing.

Yes, thank you.

To learn about self-love we have to go back in time to the place where we forgot it. Self-love is permission, after all. When we're kids, we give this permission to ourselves to do what we want and believe what we want.

My nephews are four and two. They don't do small talk. They exist in a world of experience and wonder, where they ask for what they want, and navigate life through their feelings. At the moment, they are their own autonomy. If they don't like something, god help you convincing them to like it.

Eventually they'll begin to install the same programming we've installed. They'll be motivated by guilt, shame, obligation and judgement, just like you and me are. They'll be convinced that their dreams are childish. They'll be shown certain well-worn paths and perhaps talked out of finding something new and unique.

But that piece of their programming has not fully uploaded yet. For now they want to bake cakes for breakfast, sell their grandmother's fruit and vegetables on the doorstep, teach the cat to speak, and show me what they can do over and over again. They love themselves and move about the world with a fearlessness because they are comfortable with this self-love.

If your life is miserable, it's likely because of your programming. You were programmed into believing that life is all about survival. It was never supposed to be fun, or even that interesting, let alone awe-inspiring.

Your journey to self-love begins with the courage to move beyond simply surviving and love your life.

HOW TO FALL IN LOVE
WITH YOUR LIFE

'Nature loves courage. You make the
commitment and nature will respond
to that commitment by removing
impossible obstacles. Dream the
impossible dream and the world will not
grind you under, it will lift you up. This is
the trick. This is what all these teachers
and philosophers who really counted,
who really touched the alchemical gold,
this is what they understood. This is the
shamanic dance in the waterfall. This is
how magic is done. By hurling yourself
into the abyss and discovering it's a
feather bed.' —Terrence McKenna

When I was about 12, I made a decision that really changed my life. I was moving to a new school, and had the option to pick art or economics as a subject.

I loved art. From four years of age I used to draw all over the walls in the hallway. I'd draw cars and planes that looked like they'd been done by Basquiat and put my name beneath them. When my mother came home, she'd say, 'Did you do that, Conor?' And I'd stare at it. I'd stare at the drawing and my name, a good C, two decent Os and a messy N and R and say, No, it wasn't me. And my mother would ask me again, and eventually I'd crumble in a flood of tears, shame and rolling on the carpet, and admit, 'Yes, I'd done it, I'm sorry, I'm so sorry.'

My mother encouraged my drawing in every area of life except when I did it on the walls. She brought home broken paintbrushes from her church group and found old doors and scrap wood for me to paint on. When I overran the edges or my shapes came out bent and broken, she'd feed me little drops of wisdom, such as that there are no straight lines in nature.

The day came. We all sat down, me, my mum and my dad, and we thought about my options. It was time to get serious. We sat around the kitchen table drinking instant coffee and talking. We were serious.

Jack Kornfield said this:

'In the end
these things matter most:
How well did you love?
How fully did you live?
How deeply did you let go?'

None of us knew this back then. When we thought about what mattered most, we imagined offices and expected incomes and pensions, and strategies for not ending up on the street. We knew nothing about letting go, but we could have written books about clinging on for dear life.

So, naturally, I chose economics.

For five years I studied economic theory, basic accountancy, household budgeting and the ins and outs of how to operate a small business, including hiring and firing, and now, on the other side of it, I can safely say I have rebelled so much over that one decision that my way with money, saving, banking is like an abstract painting, and my way with creativity is almost entirely monetary.

I avoid organising my finances, making budgets, even talking about money in a way that other people avoid mentioning the chia seeds between a stranger's teeth.

And when it comes to art, when it comes to raw, unburdened, boundless creativity, I find it close to impossible to even do a doodle unless someone else has badgered me into it.

My first therapist warned me about not having creativity in my life. 'You need to express what's inside you,' she said. 'You need to play with creativity. Creativity is the antidote to life.'

I don't blame my parents one bit. We were all born under the same cloud of economic uncertainty. Even so, every day we get to choose between economics or art, meaning we get to choose between the thing that momentarily placates the fear part of our brain and the thing that truly excites us. It might even be the shoes you buy. A sensible, modest brogue with a cushioned soul or a bright, flimsy peacock of a slipper that will last no longer than a candle in a downpour.

Be creative, be free

The way to fall in love with your own life is to not take it so seriously, and to be more like an artist.

Kurt Vonnegut said this: 'If you want to really hurt your parents ... go into the arts. I'm not kidding. The arts are not a way to make a living. They are a very human way of making life more bearable.'

I dated artists. I wanted to learn their tricks. Look at the people you're dating, and you might see the tricks you're trying to learn too. Are you dating someone laid back, or someone with confidence or good social skills? The reason you're drawn to them might be for what they can teach you. This is fine, but if you don't learn the lesson, you'll end up resenting them.

I'd eventually resent the artists. They'd come into my life, habitually late, perennially broke, hungry, always hungry, and in need of a phone charger. I'd take care of them, mend their clothes, buy their supplies, write their grants, remind them to eat, sleep, take vitamin D in winter. Instead of them teaching me to be free, they taught me how to take life even more seriously.

My first fiancée was an artist. She had so little money that it scared me to watch her count the change out of her purse at the supermarket tills. I can remember going to Paris with her for a show and her selling a painting. It sold for about €500, which was a decent amount of money for an up-and-coming artist. We went straight to Saint Germain, to the Repetto shoe store, and she insisted on spending nearly all of the money on white leather shoes, which were less durable than a cracker.

Have you ever been both and excited and scared by someone's attitude to life?

She had no savings. No worker bee skills. An education in fine arts and a wardrobe of vintage items that kept out neither rain nor wind, but she was free. Her creativity was her freedom. It was her way of navigating a world that was insecure, unstable and chaotic.

Her creativity scared me to the bones. She now lives in the jungles of Brazil with even more freedom, and even less apparent stability. She is at home in chaos, and she is very much at home when she's alone, and I still look at her with a little awe.

Get good at being alone

The key to being creative is to spend more time alone. There is something about being alone, deeply alone, and this doesn't have to be in the Amazonian jungle, it can come from simply doing things independently.

Alone and free from distractions, your dreamworld begins to make itself known again. Everything in existence began in this dreamworld. Legs, lungs, opposing digits, hot-air balloons, dance, all appeared in the imagination before they appeared in perception.

My mother worked a factory job for most of my childhood. She used to get a lift with a co-worker into the city. But in order to get to that co-worker she had to take a bus, and due to the infrequency of rural transport in Kildare in the 1990s, this meant arriving at her co-worker's home a good half an hour before the co-worker needed to get up. They came to an arrangement. The co-worker would leave her front door key under the mat and my mum would let herself in and sit in the living room for half an hour and wait. She did this every morning over many years, from 6.30am to 7am – with the lights out because my mum wouldn't as much as disturb a sleeping fly.

I asked her what she did in that time, and she'd reply that she prayed about the future. In the darkness she created a new reality for herself. Eventually she went back to school and started doing night classes. Another decade, a lot of study, some stress-related illnesses and a merciful layoff later, she now works from home as a therapist. People come and sit in her home for half an hour, or longer, and ask her how to change their lives, and her advice is the same as what got her there: get good at being alone.

At school, I remember, the worst thing someone could call you was a loner. If you wound up sitting on your own in a classroom or for lunch, the teasing was enough to make you feel like your life was over.

The bias against being alone continues as we grow up. In restaurants, waiters don't often know what to do with you if you walk in all on your own. When I worked as a waiter in New York, they'd tell us to sit solo tables away from the windows, at the back, as close to the kitchen as possible.

'Nobody will come in if they see single diners,' my boss explained. 'It makes them uncomfortable. It's just a tragic sight,' she said dramatically.

When I was a bartender, I used to feel pangs of sadness for the people who would come and sit at the counter all alone. Some of them were genuinely miserable, but others were quietly revelling in the thrill of complete autonomy.

A good friend of mine likes to go to bars on her own. She describes it as her extreme sport, because every time she does it, she gets a type of sedentary adrenalin high.

She brings a book, orders a cocktail and sits at the bar. Sometimes she just orders tea and might even bring her own teabag. She gets dressed up, like she was going on a date, but the last thing she wants to do when she goes to a bar on her own is meet other people; she does it to meet herself.

'I do it because sitting alone at a bar brings up all the demons,' she says. 'I experience a lot of the judgement that normally stays quiet. It says things like "You should be here with a man." Or that I look like a weirdo, or "Leave now, you're making people feel sad." And then I just sit with it, and slowly the borders of my judgements fade away as I get to experience all the shit talk in my head and then recognise it for what it is: old conditioning. Sitting alone and feeling the hammering of your conditioning, yet not reacting to it, is a little like placing your hand in fire and keeping it there. It feels like you are magic.'

This friend is also an artist. Her dad is a farmer, and her mother was a midwife. She grew up in a home in rural Wales, where the only things hanging on the walls were calendars. In terms of how far she's gone from the conditioning she grew up in, she's a true magician.

Fall in love with your life

I used to suffer a lot from depression. In the times before I knew anything about therapy or the practice of meditation, my cure for the floods of depression that seasonally appeared was to find someone to love me. I wasn't completely on the wrong track. Love was the answer, it just needed to come from me. It only took me about a dozen relationships to discover that piece of wisdom.

When we are in love with another person, we get a glimpse of our potential. But it's also an escape from ourselves. To fall in love with your life, you need to be entirely with yourself, and this is why it's so important to spend time alone.

It can start small, just sitting with our thoughts and accepting that, yes, judgement, guilt and sadness are there. This is how it is to be human, and that's what you are; it's what you chose to be. Go deeper. Can you feel a shallow murmur of love inside you? A love that's not related to anyone but yourself? A love that is pumping your lungs, moving your blood, sending a million messages through your body to let you know that you are alive?

There are no straight lines in nature. There's no obligation, judgement, shame or guilt in nature either, just appreciation for this one, magical creative explosion that is your life.

Go and paint your own picture.

THE TRUTH

Once or twice a year I go on retreat. A retreat is how you can drop out of society without giving up all your things for ever. Your relationships can still continue in the background. Your out of office reply can handle it.

The sacrifice is low.

On retreat you make commitments. One commitment is to telling the truth. You make a vow to be honest. Frankly, it's a very easy vow. Retreats are silent. How are you going to go around talking shit if you're not talking at all?

By not opening your mouth for a week, you think you're preventing all fibbing, but if I know anything about honesty, most of the lying we do is to ourselves. We're adept at being dishonest about what we really want, what we really need. Particularly in relationships.

If we want to bring peace into our lives, we need to come clean with ourselves.

Do what YOU want

I smile at the people who scare me. I apologise to folks who bump into me. I remind companies of overdue invoices with 'Apologies for spamming you but hope you don't mind paying me if it's not too much hassle'.

We are all people-pleasers to some extent. It's an important part of our evolutionary biology. If the folks around you like you, then your chances of survival are higher. But people-pleasing detaches us from our innate self. Our innate self is the part of us beyond guilt, shame, obligation and judgement: the four horsemen of the personality apocalypse.

People-pleasing is a useful piece of programming when our communities grow to the hundreds and thousands and we need to deal with each other, but at micro-levels, in intimate relationships this people-pleasing is a type of dishonesty and feeds the programming that we are trying to wake up from.

What do you want to do?

I'm happy to do whatever you want to do.

But don't you have a preference?

So long as you're happy, I'm happy.

Mooji, the Jamaican spiritual teacher, says: 'If you make human company too important you will not discover your true Self.' To disconnect from people-pleasing, sometimes we have to just disconnect from people.

I like to holiday alone. I'll take off every now and then with some books and go to a city where I don't know anyone. I walk a lot on these holidays, and it's in these moments that I find myself most honest.

Without company, I eat whatever I want to eat. With no agenda, I walk where I want to go. And with no obligation I reconnect to what my innate self needs. As it turns out, what he mostly wants to do is sit outside coffee shops and people-watch. Now and again, he'll want cake. If he passes a local football pitch, he has to stop and can't walk on until someone's taken a shot. Sometimes he wants naps.

If I manage to please my innate self (and by removing everybody else it happens naturally), it leaves me feeling full. When you're full, your people-pleasing blossoms into an honest, loving generosity.

Greedy people aren't bad, they just don't know how to feed themselves.

Love is not a transaction

In the future we will be climbing over each other to give, because we'll understand that everything, your love, your money, your shoes, is energy, and energy must never be possessed; it must flow.

But right now, we get a lot of giving wrong.

We get giving wrong because there's a battle going on between what we think and what we really believe. In all battles, every single last one of them, what you believe will always win over what you think. When we try to do something with an inner belief that it can't be done, we're more or less tying our laces together before competing in a race.

This is fear.

What we think is not our own. Our thoughts are nothing more than atmospheric pollution, cultural infection, brainwashing and conditioning. But what we believe, what we know to be true at a visceral level, guts vibrating like a spin cycle, is the truth.

So if you're doing something generous and thinking, 'Everyone's going to see I'm the kindest, most generous soul on the planet', while simultaneously believing that you should be compensated for your giving, then you're in trouble.

We have to learn how to enjoy the giving, instead of expecting praise, or to receive something in return. Our giving can't be sticky. It can't come with terms and conditions.

This doesn't mean that we become doormats. If you're giving to a bottomless cup of a human, then you're actually just enabling them to not grow up. But if you're giving your time, your wisdom, your money, your body, whatever it is you're exchanging in a relationship, with the expectation that this will get you something on the other side, then you're missing the point.

> *Don't cook someone dinner because you want them to drive you to the airport in the morning.*

> *Don't pay for a holiday with the expectation that you can act like an asshole on that holiday and get away with it.*

> *Don't give your partner a blow job because you want him to cancel his weekend away and stay with you.*

> *Don't put up shelves in their living room and then write it down in some little book of IOUs.*

Just be honest with yourself and your partner. If you want to give, give. If you want your partner to stay for the weekend, instead of going away and having fun, ask them.

I remember a holiday in Prague with a girlfriend. She had a friend who lived in the city who'd just broken up with someone – Christ, isn't everyone always breaking up with someone? – and she wanted to get coffee with her. I said, Go, do it, not because I really wanted her to go but because I wanted her to feel guilty afterwards. I wanted her to go find her friend and leave me on my own to have a miserable time (this I would ensure), so I could then manipulate her about it later. Sick, right?

Once you start to get honest with yourself, you're going to notice all the weeds in your garden. My garden's not the kind of place you'd let a child play unattended. There are upturned rakes in the long grasses, broken glass here and there, deep, ankle-snapping holes across the lawn. I'm working on this. Constant gardeners – that's what we need to become.

Before we can even begin to think about involving other people in our lives, we have to learn how to be honest with ourselves.

Do you truly take care of yourself?

Do you actually love yourself?

Are you honestly committed to growing up?

Tell the truth

Our society is inherently deceitful. We don't give good feedback; we give positive feedback. We don't say what we feel, but we show it all the same. We don't voice our dissatisfaction and confront our problems, we have affairs. Could you imagine telling your partner that you find other people attractive? I mean, they do too, right?

I would never have written a book if it hadn't been for the radical honesty of a girlfriend of mine. At that stage of my life I wanted to be a painter. I wasn't very good, but people told me I was. Those people were trying to be kind, but really they were just lying. Pina, my girlfriend, was Italian. She spoke very directly. I'm Irish. I'm not sure I've ever spoken directly.

'Look,' she said. 'I want to tell you the truth. Your painting. It's OK, but It's not really good. Why don't you write instead? Do what comes naturally to you?'

We are racing towards maturity, although it may not always seem that way. A mature people, the ones we're growing into, are an honest people. Being honest is more natural.

Our collective honesty begins at the personal. Right now, in what ways are you kidding yourself? And how are you attempting to pull the wool over your own eyes?

As Buddha said: 'There are three things that cannot be long hidden: the sun, the moon and the truth.'

ROLE-PLAYING GAMES

If you don't think yourself worthy of love, then you'll go into every relationship pretending to be someone else until you get caught out. I dated an alcoholic, a workaholic and a person addicted to smoking weed over the space of about five years. In each relationship we were looking for something from the other person that we were not prepared to give to ourselves. This made our time together hellish.

Nobody can give to you what you can't give to yourself.

Relationships are transformative, although the change doesn't always feel so groovy. All of us turn into different versions of ourselves when we're in relationships. Folk who are incredibly confident among friends can become sensitive and insecure in romantic relationships. I know I can.

If we're going to sign up for relationships (and to be honest, I don't know how we're not), then we've got to become experts at deciphering who we are when we're in them.

'Reality is merely an illusion', said Einstein, 'albeit a very persistent one.'

Technology is catching up with us. I remember being at a party in Los Angeles many years ago and somebody gave me a set of VR goggles. It turned the living room into the surface of Mars. As I walked slowly through the crowd, I could hear people talking, and I knew where I was, but I also thought I was in space. It took a lot of work not to identify the red rocks and the hazy air around me as real.

This is how the 'real' world is. The real world is not real. It feels real, it looks real, it tastes real – especially when we're falling in and out of love – but it's not actually real.

We are, for the most part, lost in reality, actors who've forgotten the lights and the stage and the prompters in the front row and are totally engrossed in their role.

We lose ourselves when we fall in love. Love, thanks to the unique cocktail of chemicals that wrestles our body to the ground, requires that we fall asleep for a while.

It's crucial that we can fall in love without falling completely asleep. It's imperative that we can experience the thrill of love while still being aware of who is experiencing it. To know not just your little life, but your great, mysterious life too.

There is no greater time for reflection than when we are in relationship. A loving relationship gifts us the opportunity to live up close and personal with another human and see all their flaws. And they in turn get to see ours. It's in this realm that we get to see who we really are, or really think we are.

Here are some of the classic roles we play when we're playing at being in love.

My sad, empty pockets

There's an expression that a rich person is not simply a poor person with money. It means that, regardless of how much money you give to someone who has been conditioned for poverty, they will still feel a lingering lack.

I'm like this. I grew up poor, and while I have less fear of poverty now, I still find it hard to spend money like other people. I have a resistance to taking taxis. I get spooked by the price of organic vegetables. When my sister got married 10 years ago, I bought a suit in a charity shop, even though I had a full-time job at the time.

Lack is a habit. A habit is a trained behaviour. It's something you do for no reason other than it's what you've always done. Checking your phone when you wake up in the morning, the seat you take on the bus, the face you make when someone says you're looking tired, the reply you instinctively give when someone asks you to do something new.

We can bring lack to our love, too, and that never ends well. If you don't believe that you can get the love you want, then it won't be in a hurry to find you. If you don't believe that you deserve a partner who will adore you, care for you, rub your shoulders, make you tea, read you sections of this book (I recommend the chapter on intimacy) while you lie in a bubble bath, then it's not going to happen of its own accord.

If, for example, you believe all men are shit, or that women can't be trusted, then no matter what you do, no matter how many dates you go on, you will not find a decent, honest person. Not because they don't exist, but because you won't believe in them.

Life's a restaurant. The waiter will bring you whatever you ask for. You just have to make up your mind what it is you actually want.

Our minds create the world around us. They create the dream. When we're at the mercy of our minds, this world is a brutal place. We can see this all the time. If you're beautiful, intelligent and perfectly datable yet you don't see this for yourself, then even if a long line of people are waiting at your door, you won't see them.

Lack is a type of programming in our minds. Its only purpose is to get in your way. But because the programming is so intricate, so native, you begin to believe that's just the way it is.

To deactivate lack programming, first become aware of it. And whenever it appears, counter it with a barrage of positivity:

Repeat after me: I am lovable. I am beautiful. I am smart. I am successful. I am a badass. I am worthy.

The low-worth diet

Lack is different from worth, but they're so close they interchange. Lack is related to the future. What's coming down the line. What may be. But worth is related to the here and now. What you've got in your sad, empty pockets.

You might not believe this, but there is a dial inside your head. On this dial there are a number of levels. Depending on what type of brain you've come equipped with, you could have all kinds of things.

It is set to one thing. And no matter what you might think you want, or what you write in your dating profiles, or what you say to your friends, when this dial is fixed, that's what you get.

This dial is your subconscious type. Your conscious type looks a certain way, reads certain books, kisses with a tongue, has a hard or a soft body, and so on. Your unconscious type has none of these physical identifiers, because this type is all about how you feel about yourself. This dial is connected to your sense of worth.

Some people believe they are worth their weight in gold, but most of us, practically all of us, can't count more than loose change.

Some years ago, I was in a relationship with an alcoholic. I allowed her to treat me like shit, and because my worth at this stage of my life was so low, I toughed that relationship out for two years. Near the end of the relationship I took a job in Afghanistan, and after a couple of weeks of curfews, midnight skirmishes and evacuating our home for regular bomb threats, I realised that I was calmer in a war zone than I had been in a relationship with her, and we broke up.

If your worth dial is set as low as mine was then, of course this is the exact type of relationship you'll end up in. They don't have to be an alcoholic. It might just be someone who doesn't do what they say, or someone who treats you mean.

If you've found yourself in the low-worth role then you can change it. Remember, you're the director. Take a pen and paper and write down a list of things you don't want any more. They might be big red flag terms like no signs of commitment, a lack of kindness, flakiness.

Take a pen and paper and write down a
list of things you don't want any more.

When you're done, go out on the street and put your list in a metal bucket. Douse it in petrol and drop a match on top. Dancing around the bucket is optional.

Then go back inside your home and make another list of things that you *do* want. Put this list on your door, or your mirror, or the pillow beside your bed.

Now make a list of things you want
– and deserve.

If you're already in a relationship, this can still work. It will involve boundaries and some great communication, but if you change, the world changes too.

The ugly duckling

This is also related to worth. To be honest, they're all related to each other. They feed each other in the same way dry wood feeds fire. If you're working on one, you'll end up working on them all. Healing is holistic, yet it's also surprisingly economical.

How you believe yourself to look is also all about your programming. I have skinny legs. At best my white skin goes a little beige. For years I lived in hot countries and didn't wear shorts or take my T-shirt off at the beach. I hated my body. I wouldn't even walk around naked in my own home. Each time I'd catch a glimpse of myself in a mirror – and, Jesus, isn't it wild how people who don't like their reflection are always stumbling upon mirrors? – I'd feel miserable.

I really wanted my body to be beautiful, but this is the thing, bodies are never beautiful.

Buddhism goes a long way to dispel the idea that our bodies are these things of beauty. That's why its participants shave their heads and wear the same formless clothes. In monasteries, young monks, bubbling with hormones and desire, will often meditate in mortuaries. Their instructions are to meditate on the sinews, bones, bile, guts, intestines, urine, poop of a body. And if that doesn't kill their boners outright, meditate on the bacteria and the worms devouring the dead skin.

Our bodies are shitting, puking, snoring, sweating death boxes that start to break down in our early thirties. Often earlier. Believing that bodies are a source of beauty is not only wrong, but it also makes life unfair and everyone miserable.

Our beauty standards are based on bizarre, unhealthy standards that brainwash us. How often do folk make the mistake of dating someone who looks attractive, but is clearly no match for them, just because their friends will approve?

It'd be great if instead of thinking, *That's a beautiful body,* we'd think, *Isn't it beautiful what that body just did?* Caring, listening, saying something kind, humming a little song, loving, hugging, giving money to a homeless person, helping a bug climb out of the window on a sunny day – all of these are beautiful things bodies can do, but bodies themselves, these poop machines on legs, aren't beautiful. We'd all be such happy little humans if we thought like that.

Irreparable

If you're reading this book, then you are repairable. More than repairable, you're in pretty good shape. When people come to talk to me and they tell me that they're a mess, I reply, 'You couldn't be a mess if you had the energy and the motivation to try to work on yourself.' People who are really a mess can't do that. People who are really irreparable don't go looking for repair shops.

I played this role for a long time in relationships. I blamed my childhood. I blamed my chicken legs. When I first started going to therapy, I was thrilled because this confirmed for me that I was broken, but my Serbian therapist quickly pointed out that, despite how much I loved the idea that I was broken beyond repair, I had known enough love in my life to be healthy.

If you believe that there is something wrong with you, you are probably right. We are all a little messed up. But if you think you're irreparable, that's just a role you're playing.

Many of the problems we experience in relationships can be solved if we investigate ourselves rather than focusing so much of our energy on our partner. We are taught that everything is outside us, beyond our control, but if you're the actor and the director, then all you need to do, if you're not happy with your role, is delete your lines and reimagine it.

You will never really get your shit completely together. At least I hope for you that you won't. If you did, there'd be nothing to live for any more. The purpose of life is to get muddy and messy, to break up with someone and then get back together with them the same night. To fall off the wagon, get dragged behind it and then pick yourself up again.

We heal in relationships

It's important to remember that who we think we are when we think we're in love is just a role that we're playing, as we experience trauma, triggering and projections. This process is necessary. It's how you heal, and not just your life, but the intergenerational trauma that your whole family has experienced.

We have a tendency to put spiritual people on pedestals. And spiritual people have a tendency to put themselves on pedestals too – I mean, all that white clothing is just one red sock away from disaster. But it's very important to remember that holy folk, these people we revere, are just the sick people who healed, and continue to heal, themselves. There's nothing in them that couldn't be in you.

As my mother never tires of saying, especially when her son is crying down the phone, we heal in relationships. She's right, just don't forget who you really are when you're in one.

SURRENDER

*'Surrender is the ultimate sign of strength
and the foundation for a spiritual life.
Surrendering allows us to return to
our true nature and move effortlessly
through the cosmic dance called life.'*
—Debbie Ford

There's a point in everyone's life where we're forced to surrender. It happens in our love stories, where we realise that we can no longer control the direction, we can just try our best to move with it. It happens with psychedelics, when we recognise that holding on to normal states of consciousness will just prolong the fear and anxiety. And it happens again in meditation, when we experience the futility of trying to solve thoughts, and instead we just sit back and become aware of them.

If you're trying to solve the problem of your life, the most loving thing you can do is just sit back and become aware of it instead. This is how we value ourselves.

'To offer our hearts in faith means recognising that our hearts are worth something, that we ourselves, in our deepest and truest nature, are of value,' says Sharon Salzberg.

There is value in every part of you. You honour that by being alone and bringing awareness to everything you do. You sweep nothing under the carpet, because it's all you.

To live in full awareness is to live in love. Love might seem like a feeling, but to live in love, to choose love as your way of life, means that love is no longer a feeling with the capacity to come and go, it's actually a state of mind.

What this means in practice is that instead of waiting for love to come to you, you go to it. It's a matter of evolution, or manifestation – whether you want something enough to evolve into it.

Insect world

About 125 million years ago, there were no flying insects. Insects at that time either crawled or climbed, and for the most part none of them could see anything wrong with that. But there were creatures who lived high in trees, and depended upon the trees for their existence. Climbing up and down trees took effort. But at opportune times, when the wind blew or the trees swayed, they discovered that they could let go of one tree and just glide through the air to another.

Can you imagine the first insect that did this? Perhaps it happened by accident and the wind just snatched her free. Did she scream as she let go of the trunk? Did she picture a chilling death at the foot of the tree? Or perhaps she'd really wanted it, perhaps this insect, inspired by a leaf in flight, had manifested this transformation, and now she couldn't believe that it had actually paid off. Over time this insect got better at jumping. Good enough that she taught others. Soon all the insects were jumping between treetops, and the days of crawling up and down to the bottom of each tree were just a distant memory.

Fast forward another million years and these insects were no longer dependent upon wind, or a favourable bend in the bough; these insects had grown wings, and could fly.

Buddha was maybe not the first human to let go of the tree, but he left us with the best example of how a human can evolve from an organism that waits patiently for love to an organism that is just love. Depression was his fuel, and enlightenment was his first flight.

There are many tales about his life that are simply myth. One of them goes that shortly after his birth, he stood up, took seven steps and proclaimed, 'I will end suffering in the world'. A baby has just come out with a sentence like that, and the onlookers are calm enough to remember how many steps he took?

Buddha wasn't superhuman. A simple insect wanted wings and a simple human wanted to live in love. Neither of these beings were magical, but they were magical in their depth of creativity.

En-lighten-ment

The subtle sign that you're falling in love is a gentle feeling of peace. Your problems shrink. You feel somehow more whole. The wanting, the longing that bothered you before is nowhere to be found. Briefly, because the feeling associated with romantic love is always short, we walk around on a cloud, and there is something untouchable about us.

When I've been in love, in the early, dreamy days, I've got bad news that just washed right through me. I reversed a rental car into a small stone wall, in love, possibly because of love, and the thousand-euro excess fee was like water off a duck's back for me. If that had caught me any of the other 40-something weeks of the year when I was not feeling peak love levels, it would have made me sick to the belly.

This is what happens when you are in love. It's similar to what happens when we spend long periods training our minds. If you stumbled into the grounds of a silent retreat on the last day just before the signal to start talking again, you'd say, Look at all these people, they must be in love.

By increasing our awareness, we can transform from being in love to something more sustainable and practical; we can just be love. You can choose love as your way of life.

This is what Buddha meant when he talked about enlightenment. Think about that word: en-lighten-ment. You're being injected with lightness, dropping the heavy baggage, learning to fly – doesn't that sound a little like love?

Our future is dependent on us harnessing the feeling of being in love so that we can learn to simply be love.

Ego is a trap

In this book I talk a lot about addictions. Gabor Maté describes addiction as 'any behaviour that a person finds temporary pleasure or relief in and therefore craves, suffers negative consequences from, and has trouble giving up'.

According to this definition, we're all addicted to thinking. Our lives are dominated by our thoughts, and this makes us miserable; the consequence of this is that we're unable to love. Strong thoughts can make us do some of the worst things imaginable. At a macro level, these strong thoughts are the reason we're destroying the planet, but at a micro level they're the reason we self-sabotage, we isolate, and we shut ourselves off from the one thing that would ensure our healing: love.

Buddha's enlightenment, his awakening to love, was his realisation that the ego is a trap. We all know this. We can see it in others. It's impossible to miss a runaway ego. You know how it is when we watch a couple fighting. Two egos duking it out for superiority. The ego must always take a position. It must be right. At the heart of any ego drive is a need for power. This appears like power over others, but it's actually power over you. We're addicted to thoughts because of the overwhelming power that our egos have over us.

Carl Jung said that where there is an abundance of power there will be a scarcity of love.

Buddha's enlightenment was his realisation that you don't have to identify with the ego, you don't have to identify with thoughts, you can just be aware of them.

We do this by no longer trying to run away from ourselves. We surrender to the reality as it is and the potential that may come, a potential to love beyond your wildest dreams.

Maybe even love everyone.

Part 4
Them

LOVE BIG, LOVE OFTEN

One of my closest friends is my neighbour in Berlin. Without her I don't know where I'd be. She's also a meditator. To be honest, she's more disciplined than me. Each morning at 6.30am she knocks on my door, and we meditate in my living room together for an hour. If she didn't do this, I mean, if I didn't get the knock, there are plenty of mornings when I wouldn't have got my ass out of bed. I am nothing without my friends.

Afterwards we drink coffee and chat. We've been doing this for a few years now, and we know quite a lot about each other. Conversations after meditation are almost always more honest than all other conversations. When you've meditated, you penetrate through so many of the illusory layers of your life that it would feel absurd to lie or gloss over details. We can see clearly again; why would you want to muddy that water? We talk a lot about our meditation after meditation.

'How was it for you?'

'Hard work. You?'

'Not so bad. My thoughts were kind of dense.'

But we also talk about our parents. They are, after all, the reason we meditate, the reason we have pain to work out.

Her father and mother fell in love when they were both young. They were hippies in the 1960s, the first generation after the Nazis. Now that was a highly traumatised generation. They hated their parents. They hated Germany. We think that the social justice warriors of our time are something new, but each generation has had its own team of attack dogs, dismantlers, aggressive truth-sayers.

My friend was born in a commune. When her mother was just five months pregnant, her father stood up at a group meeting and said, in front of everybody, that he didn't love her any more. He didn't feel it, and wanted to share this with the group, to be open and honest. This shook my friend's mother so hard that my friend can still feel it nearly 40 years later.

He didn't feel it any more, what could he do?

A relationship is not a race to be won,
it is an organic being to be nourished,
pruned, watered and helped to flourish
in whichever way it needs.

Love is work

You can do a lot, as it turns out. Love is never a feeling. As C.S. Lewis said, 'Love is not affectionate feeling, but a steady wish for the loved person's ultimate good as far as it can be obtained.'

Love is work. Love is action. Sure, we feel love now and again. Romantically we might even feel it solidly for the first six to nine months of a relationship. I know I have. It's within that blissed-out time frame that I've made most of the curious life choices that have shaped my travels.

You're moving to Italy for someone you don't know that well? But it feels so good.

Love has to be independent of feeling. In fact, it's often despite the feeling. The moments when we don't feel love are the moments when we get the choice to activate it or not. It's about making the decision to treat somebody like they are important to you.

Love, the feeling – the bubbling cocktail of hormones, the silly juice that makes you proclaim wild things, drive stupid distances, scale balconies in the Veronese night and swallow poison – is not genuine love.

Genuine love is action, commitment and wisdom. If you want to love other people, you have to tick those three boxes. Wisdom comes from presence, and presence comes from attention and attention is the hardest work when attention is the one thing this society wants to take from you.

To truly love another person we have to learn to rebel against the individualistic programming of our society and truly give our time to another.

Thank you, Patsy McArthur

Most of us can think of examples from our life where we felt the attention of somebody else, where we became aware that somebody, with no other intention than love, was trying to understand us. If it wasn't our parents, then maybe it was a relative. Perhaps even a teacher. Maybe even a neighbour.

I can think of many examples from when I was a kid, but one stands out from later in my life. I was in a bar at two in the morning talking to an older woman who was visiting town and had come here with a friend. She was a serious artist. She had a studio. She had a gallery. One of her paintings hung in the Portrait Gallery in London. Her parents weren't paying her rent; she was the real deal. I was talking to her about writing and telling her that I wanted to make books. I had ideas, I told her.

'Ideas are nothing,' she said to me. 'You need to work.'

In a smoky bar, with no hope of getting up early, she gave me a dressing down.

'Who are all these people?'

'My friends,' I said.

'They're not your friends. They don't care about you. They don't want you to succeed. All they care about is that you don't leave them,' she told me.

She was right, by the way. I don't see any of those people who were in the bar that night any more.

She told me that if I didn't stop drinking and start working I'd never even get close to writing books.

'Go home', she said, 'sober up. Take yourself seriously.'

'Right now?'

'Yes. Just go, don't say goodbye or they'll pull you back.'

I got up, left a half pint, took my coat, went home and wrote for an hour. The next morning she called me and told me I needed to write for eight hours that day. I complained that I had lunch plans. 'Cancel them,' she said.

For a week, she took time to call me and coerce me every day until her attention, her wisdom and her love had enabled me to get into a routine and make a start on a book. That book was called *Saint Frank*. It didn't make me a penny, but it made me so damn proud of myself.

I don't talk to that artist any more. She came into my life for little more than a week, and for some reason – some great karmic chance – she decided to love me, and it made such a difference.

Her name was Patsy McArthur. If you're reading this, Patsy: thank you.

We are taught that love is spontaneous, wild, impulsive and all-consuming. This education sets us up for so much misery. Love is wisdom. Love is work. Love is the constant and arduous task of paying attention to someone else and trying to figure out what they need. It's neither discriminatory nor judgemental. It's more like the sun in the sky than Romeo, half-cut on a Veronese balcony.

Love is:

How can I help?

What do you need?

I'm listening, what do you want to say?

We all just want to be loved

David Graeber was an anarchist. Anarchists are not, as popular belief has it, against everything. They are often just pro-human, and believe that without rules, controls and hegemonic forces, humans would not butcher and kill each other; they'd cooperate.

He said this: 'The ultimate hidden truth of the world is that it is something we make and could just as easily make differently.'

We can make the world very different, and we will. That's our future. That's the new earth. It requires us to learn how to love despite what we feel, and to recognise that love is wisdom, attention and a commitment to understanding the fellow travellers we meet on this planet.

The fellow travellers you do meet are just as fragile, needy and broken as you. When they look in the mirror, they're met with doubts. When they open their mouth to talk about themselves, they feel insecure and judged. Loneliness and failure follow them just like they follow you. When we can recognise this, then we can also recognise that not only can we love everyone, but we have to love everyone.

As Ram Dass said, in the end, we're all just walking each other home.

BLAME YOUR PARENTS

'The past has no power to stop you from being present now. Only your grievance about the past can do that.'
—*Eckhart Tolle*

Love is the highest frequency.

When they stick monks in MRI scans, the one practice that lights up nearly all their brains is the practice of generating love. If you can meet everyone and everything with love, then your life will shine and blossom and grow just like a laboratory monk.

But of course we don't do this. You and I are a lot of things, but we're not that, especially not on Mondays. Especially if you don't call us back when you said you would.

The reason we don't shine bright all the time is our parents. They fuck us up a little bit. Sometimes they fuck us up an awful lot – in a way that is actually their job, or their role. Childhood is a gauntlet. Even the most ideal of family situations is a petri dish for pain, trauma and the dysfunctional habits we grow into as adults.

When we begin to look at our childhoods, it inevitably brings up a whole bunch of bad feelings. Resentment, powerlessness and abject resignation are difficult because they're related to things that happened, that can't unhappen. It would make you cry.

One way to end the tears is to imagine that sure, they were your makers, but you were always in charge. This is how you do that.

Even if it's not true, if you're trying to make sense of your family, try to imagine that you've chosen them. Picture yourself in the waiting room between lives being guided round various family constellations by an eager saleswoman trying to make her monthly quota. Two more sales and she automatically triggers her bonus. She's got vim.

Let me introduce you to the Daddy Issues Package, she says, opening up the brochure on a fresh life. *Your dad will leave you aged three. Your relationship with your mom will be complicated. Subconsciously you'll always believe that she drove him away and you'll resent her. You'll also have horrible luck with men. Drummers, addicts, gamers. By some fluke, at a friend's wedding, you'll finally meet Floyd.*

He looks great, you might say.

He is great, she'll reply, *but something will be missing, and you'll chase him away.*

Really?

Really. You thought he was too nice. You end up recognising your pattern and accepting your life in the end, but not until you're in your late seventies. The last ten years, barring a couple of cancer scares and two replacement hips, are a cake walk. And you have a cat.

What's the lesson from this life, then?

The lesson from this life is to not punish yourself for a parent's lack of love.

OK, what about this one on the next page? That looks lovely.

This is a popular life. It's the Little House on the Prairie *Package. Your parents will adore you. Your siblings will be your best friends. You'll do great at school and marry your childhood sweetheart, a carpenter, who, I won't lie, has wood skills in the bedroom too, wink wink.*

Does anything bad happen to me in this life?

Yes. Something horribly traumatic.

What is it?

Your dog runs away, but he comes back again three days later.

Oh, so what do I learn?

Not much, actually. This is more of an entry-level life if I'm being honest.

What about this one? There aren't many pictures.

That's a particularly tough life. Expert level. Not many people buy this one. You die before you're even five from a rare, uncurable disease.

That's horrible.

It is. You're a happy baby, but you're also in a lot of discomfort, and some pain.

What do I learn in that life?

You learn how to give and you teach your family how to love under extreme circumstances.

So how are you doing? Do you think you've had an entry-level life or an expert-level life so far? Has it been dull, or have you cried a bathtub of tears, fooled yourself, given up, started again and learned some hard-won lessons?

Even if you've not done much more than spend your life in the town where you were born, and met the same people over and over again, you will still have experienced fear and loss and grief and heartache and great disappointments. Even if you're bored of it all, that's still part of a plan. Like a haphazard collection of airport barriers, leading you through a series of perpetual sharp turns, the problems you encounter in your life are not there just to frustrate you, they're in place to get you where you need to go.

You say childhood, I say bootcamp

Everything begins at home. The relationship we have with our parents is repeated in shades, variants and all-too-familiar ways in every other relationship we enter. We fall in love with eerily precise yet strangely sexy versions of our parents all the time.

Ever met someone who was a bit different, who your friends couldn't understand, who you couldn't even understand and yet you found yourself texting, flirting and convincing your way into a relationship with them?

I don't know what it is about him, but that moustache just sings to me, and the way he only answers one from three texts makes me feel like a child again.

Look a little closer under the hood and you might discover that the relationship model on offer is actually a clever repackaging of the one you had as a child.

I remember once upon a time having a breakthrough after a couple's therapy session and announcing to my then partner that the way she loved me reminded me of my dad.

'It all makes sense now,' I told her as we ate hamburgers on our laps, part of our post-therapy drive-thru treat. 'My love for you is an attempt to reconnect with him. When you reject me sexually, it's not really you I'm upset with, it's him!'

She looked at me aghast, sucked hard on her soda, and we never had sex again.

If you can learn to understand your folks, and you're slightly more judicious than me about when you share that information, you'll begin to understand every relationship you've ever had.

Our parents, their relationships, their dreams, their struggles, offer unique clues to our own.

Buddha said this: 'There are no bad people, only bad behaviour.'

Your parents screw up because they are also screwed up. This isn't a flaw, it's a design.

Earth is a planet, but it's also a type of school.

Childhood is a very carefully engineered stage of our development designed to shake our trust in other people, encourage the growth of an individual ego and give us something to work with, or work against, for the rest of our time on the planet. This is our schooling.

Buddhists don't believe in a soul. For them, the parents you get is related to your karma, your good work in past lives. By the way, if you've somehow stumbled upon this book without really seeking it out, then that would be considered good karma too. The idea is that you've chosen everything. There is a part of you, a part that you can sense but are not always in direct contact with, that has tailor-made this life just for you.

Everything you encounter is intended for your spiritual advancement – including your parents.

For many years I believed I was adopted. My parents even joked about it. 'Yes, we found you on the side of the dual carriageway in a cardboard box.' The story suited me fine, actually. It was easier than seeing the connection between me and my parents, because I didn't want to see myself in them. I didn't want to love the people who had hurt me.

Of all the characters we're given to love in this life, it's our parents who are often the trickiest.

I've found that the best way to make peace with my parents has been to study them very carefully. They're part of the ingredients that make you. Your relationship choices, your self-esteem, your attachment style, your preferences for food, how you dress, whether you think you can dance or sing. Even the ways in which you rebelled, the careful efforts you've made to grow distinct from your family, were influenced by your family.

I lived in Berlin for all of my thirties. My friends are all from other parts of the world. Most of us, if not pretty much all of us, had uncomfortable childhoods that compelled us to leave our lands. I know I'm healing now because I'm spending so much more time in Ireland.

Getting to know your parents is an incredible way to get to know yourself. Imagining that you've chosen them, that their teaching was all a part of a loving, brilliant plan conceived by you, is an incredible way to come to peace with your upbringing.

Some years ago, I was in a relationship with an alcoholic. On our first date, I had to help her to her home, get her in her door and put her to bed, because she was too drunk to stand up.

If I'd had different parents, I'm not sure if I would have been so attracted to the unpredictable love she was offering, but there was something about her scattered conversations, her neediness, her romantic fatalism and her inability to show up, think straight or take care of any of my needs that seemed familiar. She felt like home.

Writing this, I can distinctly remember how she tasted. The alcohol came out of her pores. It hung on her lips like gloss. The air in her bedroom on a Sunday morning was flammable. I'd ask her if she'd been drinking the night before and she'd fly into a rage, calling me sanctimonious, mister goody two shoes, perfect Conor. In these moments, something strange, something unimaginable would happen; I'd fall into a strange, confused, quiet place and apologise.

You always make me feel bad, she'd say, and I'd apologise again then go to the corner shop, buy orange juice, eggs and bread and fix her breakfast while she had a bath and a cry. On the way to and from the shop, I'd beat myself up – *Why can't you just be cool, man? Why do you have to be so judgemental?*

This is gaslighting. It's a type of emotional manipulation. The person acting out makes you believe that you're the one actually acting out. If you're the sort of person with the tendency to doubt yourself, and don't always know if you're in the right or the wrong, then it's so important to have good people around you. It's important to be surrounded by love or have it close at hand. At the time I had no one. It was only when a friend visited and joined us in a bar one night, and watched as my girlfriend drank her glass, then my glass, then his, and asked, 'What are you doing with this person?' that the penny finally dropped.

Dependency? Never heard of it

A big habit pattern in my life has been to date the self-destructive. I have a kind of radar for it. If there were a relationship Olympic Games, then my event would be the 'co-dependency steeplechase'.

Heavy drinkers, heavy smokers, workaholics, people who would forget to feed themselves, partners in massive debt, people on the verge of breakdowns, folk going through a wobble – I have a preternatural ability to spot them, even beneath a well-constructed veneer of adulting.

The line running between them all has nothing to do with them and everything to do with me: ultimately, I was choosing partners who could never meet my needs, thereby confirming a bias that I'd established in childhood, that the people you love can't take care of you. Yikes.

Perhaps you can relate. We are attracted to the familiar. The familiar means that they are well-known. If you meet someone and they seem familiar, this most likely means that they remind you of your family.

In his essay 'Why You Will Marry the Wrong Person', Alain de Botton makes the bold claim that we are attracted to the people most suited for our healing, not our happiness.

My mother likes to say, whenever I come home with the pieces of another broken heart, offering them to her in a way your cat might offer you a half-tortured bird or mouse, 'We're damaged in relationships, and we heal in relationships.'

It's her kind way of saying, *Well, this is what you ordered on the menu, love.*

It's your story, and it's not finished yet

If you're in a relationship with someone right now, it might be useful to put this book down for a second and ask yourself: What is it they do that irritates you? What do they say that brings out anger in you, or intense sadness, and something worse than either of those relatively clear-cut emotions, confusion – the nagging sense that there's something not quite right, something you can't understand?

And from that, it would be even more useful to trace a line from their behaviour, and, more important, your reaction to their behaviour, back to your parents.

What bugs you? What gets under your skin? Think about it for a moment. Can you identify where this feeling, thought or behaviour might have come from?

If one of your parents was an alcoholic, yes, this might predispose you to dating alcoholics, but it also might make you extra sensitive to even moderate drinking in your partner. After I emerged from my relationship with an alcoholic, I saw alcoholics everywhere. I couldn't go on a date with someone without counting the millimetres of wine, the rate of ingestion, the micro-changes in personality.

There's an interesting cliché regarding therapy. First you learn that you hate your parents, and then you learn to understand them, and finally, with luck and persistence and depending on circumstances, you might even learn to love them again, in the way you did in your first years on the planet.

Learning to love your parents again is the key to improving your current relationships. If you can manage to step back from the intense emotions surrounding childhood and see your parents as just deeply flawed people, you can begin to make sense of how they acted the way they did.

Buddha said, 'If you truly loved yourself, you couldn't hurt another.'

If your parents hurt you, you can rest assured that someone hurt them too.

Meditation teaches us how to remove ourselves from the punishing cycle of thinking that leaves us miserable. It helps us climb free from the stories that dictate our moods. How your childhood was is also a story. And like all good stories, your story is dramatic, meaning there's suspense, tragedy, sadness, near misses, and so much feeling. But do remember that it's your story, and it's not finished yet.

Your story is a collection of thoughts. If you're very still, you can watch the story telling itself into existence over and over again. It comes out in blanket statements that we make about ourselves. But our stories don't have to be death sentences; they can also be challenges.

> *If you grew up in a home where there was fear, can you become a beacon of safety?*

> *If you grew up surrounded by scarcity, can you, despite this, grow generous, giving and free?*

> *If your parents didn't touch you enough, can you become open, tactile, warm and heart-centred?*

You can work on the story you've had with your family. Whether you chose expert-level or just intermediate, your pathway to peace is to accept the script you've been given and work with it.

What matters is that you heal

Our childhood is a kind of bootcamp. A shocking, unsettling couple of decades where we're sensitive and impressionable, and the words people say penetrate us like injections.

I can't eat an apple or pear without a slight twinge of worry that if I accidentally swallow a seed, a tree might grow in my gut. The same goes for chewing gum or leaving the house with wet hair. I don't know anyone who's died from either, but the teaching runs deep: wet hair and I'll die of pneumonia and chewing gum in my stomach will cause a gastric eruption like the breakfast scene in *Alien*.

Our role as adults is to make sense of this bootcamp, make sense of our parents and, in this way, make sense of ourselves. Trust your authority. Trust that everything you've experienced happened for a reason, and that that reason is your own personal growth.

In the waiting room between lives, in that timeless space, piped music, lavender in the air, windows that look out onto any view you desire, free refreshments and a bathroom so clean that it explodes and rebuilds itself after each use, you chose a certain kind of life. It doesn't matter which one. What matters is that you heal from it.

With each life we are offered dignity, love and hope if we can learn from and grow through our pain.

There's a teaching in Buddhism that all of our ancestors and all future generations are present in us all the time. If that's true, then all you need to do is heal your heart and in one fell swoop you're healing everyone who made you and everyone who will come through you. By healing yourself, you can heal your whole family.

YOUR SOULMATES
MIGHT BE YOUR MATES

*'The soul of friendship is located
in honesty, respect, sharing, and
loyalty. The making and the keeping of
friends over the long haul of a lifetime
is a spiritual practice requiring large
reserves of diligence, patience, and
nurturing.' —Eugene Kennedy*

If I'm falling in love, you might not hear from me. In those early days, when I'm dizzy with excitement and nerves and that ferocious energy that could either destroy you or make you anew, I can be out of reach. I'll miss texts, I'll cancel appointments, I'll be unreachable for long weekends. I'll be as contactable as a Starman.

I've got a handle on most of the other addictions I've had in life. I can say no to drugs, alcohol and even Instagram when I want to, but love, the first flurries of attraction, gets me every time, and inevitably it's my friends who suffer. I sometimes forget about love for my friends when I'm flowing in the fast waters of love for a new partner. It's something we all do to varying degrees, and something we all need to work on.

We can have a tendency to abandon our friends when a new lover comes along. It's almost accepted behaviour, which doesn't make it right.

I can remember one night in East London, visiting a friend who lived in Bow. We were at Fabric, the club, when he got talking to a girl and decided to go home with her. At three in the morning, with no knowledge of London, with the sense of direction of a paper plane, and in the days before smartphones, I offered to walk home so he could spend time with this complete stranger.

Naturally, I got lost and had to sleep at a bus stop in Stoke Newington. If you've ever had to spend a night at a London bus stop, you'll know that they're actually designed so you cannot. You get half an ass cheek on them at best. There's no way to lie down. If you do sleep, it's in blocks of short minutes before your body slips onto the ground again. When I eventually found my way back the next day, he was already there.

'Good night?'

'Nah.'

When I was in my twenties this felt like acceptable friend behaviour. I was guilty of doing the same too. Older, and many, many nights in clubs and potential lovers later, I'm beginning to realise that all the poetry, the flowers, the sprawling text conversations, the mixtapes and, more recently, Spotify playlists, might have been better used in the service of friend love rather than romantic love.

This is a trap I fall into. Perhaps we all do. Friends find someone new, and they disappear, only to return when that new feeling changes to the old feeling of hurt and confusion. Life is a cycle of mini deaths and births, and friendship doesn't escape that pattern. We need to get better at it.

With a little help from my friends

Friendship, more than family, more than partners, will be the most important relationship of the future. More than your job, more than your house, more than your money in the bank, the one thing we will need to survive upon this planet will be a loving community.

Your soulmate, the person who gets you, the person who understands you more than anyone ever has, who makes you feel seen and heard, might actually be your mate. If you've done the work – I mean if you've chosen wisely, surrendered a little and found folks who are not afraid to call you out, hold your hand and remind you of just how great you are when you've forgotten – then you can depend on them almost as much as you depend upon yourself. This is true friendship. This is abundance.

Peering into a future where marriage is no longer for ever, fertility is not what it used to be and climate change could mean us all retreating to high ground in our golden years, your friends are one of the only sources of security.

There is an old Indian word for a friendship that includes a strong spiritual bond. The word is 'sangha'. Sangha are your friends who keep you on the right path, the ones who will hold your feet to the fire and remind you of your intentions. They're the people who will encourage you to quit your job or call you when you've got back with your ex again, and say things like *I know, I get it, we're all lonely, winter's longer than usual, life's a ghost train, but you can and will do better.*

Once upon a time, Buddha was asked about the importance of sangha by his assistant, Ananda. Ananda said,

'I get it, sangha is 50 per cent of the path,' and Buddha, ever ready with the quips, replied, 'No, Ananda, it's 100 per cent.' Your friends, according to Buddha, are more important than anyone else in your life.

Friends, if you chose them wisely, can function as a type of early warning system and a disaster relief fund, strong buffers against the inevitable disastrous life choices that you will repeatedly try to make.

Friends help you grow

After our parents, and long before a partner arrives and turns our world upside down, it's our friends who become our next teachers about love. Without them we miss out on a huge area of personal development.

When we are infants, our egos are at their tyrannical peak. We can see so clearly how powerful a baby's ego is because they experience a kind of amputation agony when objects are removed from their reach. Someone takes the car keys back and the baby starts bawling like their leg's been dropped in hot wax.

Grown-ups do this too. It can feel very embarrassing when you see a grown-up, in an airport, in traffic, waiting in line at a restaurant, wailing because something has not

We put so much weight on romantic relationships, when in truth, the great loves of many of our lives will be our good friends.

gone their way. Maturing is about not trying to make everything go your way, but instead allowing things to unfold around you with no greater personal involvement than a radio in the background.

The next time something doesn't go your way, ask yourself, why should it?

If the purpose of life is to wake up from the delusion of permanence, then things constantly going your way only strengthens that delusion. When we're confronted by the unreliability of the world, we're forced to leave the beaten track and explore the nature of reality.

A true friend will walk with you on the path. If you nourish the right kind of friendships in your life, friendships that are not afraid of telling you what you need to hear, you'll be reminded of your purpose the many times you forget.

Friends tell you when you're wrong

In Buddha's time, and perhaps in our time too, but I don't know, there were meditators who had practised so hard they had magic powers. What were the magic powers? They could read minds, visit other realms of existence and pass right through the walls. I like to imagine some could skip lines outside nightclubs.

But according to Buddha, the most powerful super-power, more powerful even than flying, is mastering our thought perceptions. Our thoughts are collective and biased, and the only way to coexist with a thinking brain is, as Eckhart Tolle often says, to observe your thoughts, but to not believe them.

The most common thought we believe is I'm right and you're wrong.

We go through life sorting the things we encounter into right or wrong. If we could do away with the reflex to classify things as right and wrong, we'd probably also do away with war, and painful break-ups, and we'd create space for growth, and freedom.

It feels good to be right. When I worked as a journalist – I knew I shouldn't but sometimes couldn't help myself – I'd scroll beneath my article to the comments section. I can remember sitting at home on my bed with a bottle of wine, weeping as I read the snarky, fact-correcting comments left by complete strangers. It felt so good for them to be right, and it felt so bad for me to be wrong.

When a more intelligent, gracious civilisation eventually stumbles upon planet Earth and can't decide whether to befriend the human population or obliterate us for our own good, the strongest argument against maintaining our existence will be the comments section in online publications.

But what exactly in you feels good when you're right? This is an interesting question to explore the next time the sensation visits. Doesn't feeling right also feel a little hollow? And if you look a little deeper, doesn't feeling right also feel just a tad lonely? It's pretty exposed and fairly isolated at the top of self-righteous mountain.

Your friends, if you've chosen wisely, will tell you when you're wrong. This is the work. We often imagine that a friendship will be fluid, while our relationships will bring the challenges. But true friendship will challenge too. True friendship will make you work. Anywhere you see the word 'work' in connection with relationship, you can also just use the word 'love'. It's the same thing. Work is simply compromise, adjusting, accepting, conceding, all the things that relinquish, if just a little, the ego's addiction to being correct.

If somebody is hurting, nobody is right

If you're very quiet and very still you might even recognise the ego as you read this. It is the part of you that feels compelled to take a stance. The little voice that can't be quiet. The part of you that is reading these paragraphs and remembering examples, keeping records, feeling every offence over and over again – that's your ego. The ego is a restless hunter. It survives on thoughts of becoming, and the feeling of being right. The ego is a lot like a voracious disease, or a golem – weak but determined as all hell.

Be very careful of feeding your need to be right.

I lost my best friend because I needed to be right. As far as pivotal moments in my life went, it was as traumatising as the end of any romantic relationship. We had worked together, we had lived together, we had travelled all over the world together, and I had begun, as many of us do, when we see people all the time, to take him for granted.

My problem with this friendship is I'd forgotten to put myself in my friend's shoes. I was flaky, unreliable and pivoting from one dramatic situation to the next. Drama, you might have noticed from your own life, is a little like a leaky pen. It spills everywhere.

At the time I was in an energy-intensive relationship. It took pretty much all my time just to keep going. I felt like I was living beneath an active volcano. In fairness, she might have felt the same way. We were both unemployed and living together in a tiny spot and couldn't manage to accept the reality of our situation, so we blamed each other.

At the same time, this best friend of mine was getting married and, broke and worn down by days of continuous fighting, I just didn't show up. I announced it less than two weeks before the wedding. It was a shitty move, but I had created an argument in my head that was so watertight that I felt justified in not only missing the wedding but also requesting that he postpone the event until I was in a better place.

I'm happy to say that in the intervening years we've rebuilt what we had, but it took a lot of wrestling, and good friends putting their neck on the line to suggest maybe I'd got it wrong, for me to understand that I wasn't right. This is a good rule of thumb: If somebody in the relationship is hurting, then nobody is right.

Love in action

Our egos are like veils of smoke that cloud our vision. It makes it almost impossible to see the full picture. The only way to see the full picture is to step back from your ego, and that means stepping back from the sense of identity we have. A way to do this is to imagine you are observing your life from a bird's eye view and attempting to observe the story unfolding in front of you without inserting yourself in it.

Imagine you are observing your life from a bird's eye view. Try to observe the story unfolding in front of you without inserting yourself in it.

The ego always wants to insert itself. The ego's function is self-invention. Children do this. They demand to be heard. The way they relentlessly interrupt stems from the ego's fear of being ignored. This is a necessary part of a kid's development, but as adults we have to learn to outgrow the grip of our egos.

If you're reading this book right now, it's safe to say you are waking up from the grip of the ego over you. If the ego had a stronger hold upon you, trust me, you wouldn't get through as much as a page. You might not have even made it past the cover. This book would make you angry. You'd turn that anger back at the person who told you about it. You'd build an elaborate story in which you were very right and everyone else was very wrong.

Waking up from the spell of ego is daunting. It can feel extremely lonely, and this is why our friendships are so important.

As I wrote this chapter, I got a phone call from a friend I went to a retreat with five years ago. We sat side by side for ten days and never spoke a word. On the last day, when we finally spoke, he asked for my number. 'You and I meditated for more than a hundred hours together,' he said. 'Our atoms are practically fused.'

We call each other up in times of need, when my life's become a little overly dramatic, and the same for him. The phone call I got while writing this chapter was just that. He had fallen in love with someone who didn't love him back, and he was suffering, and this suffering had caused him to forget to meditate and begin drinking heavily again.

'Let's meditate,' I said.

For 20 minutes we meditated on a WhatsApp call.

Stephen Batchelor writes that 'True friends are like midwives who draw forth what is waiting to be born. Their task is not to make themselves indispensable but redundant.'

A true friend is love in action.

Look around you

We're in the middle of a shift these days. I know this sounds like magical thinking, but right now, in our lives, we're birthing a new type of society. We have to. We've brought ourselves to a tipping point, where the only option is to radically change – or perish. Money, gender, conventional things like marriage, everybody having children, buying property, a job for life – all these foundational features of modern society are collapsing.

Increasingly, your friend circle will be made of people who are on the same wavelength as you. Being on the same wavelength means people who are on the same path as you. Friends who share your sense of values. Your sense of values is under constant attack from the mainstream wanting culture. Your friends will help you protect it.

The monks where I first studied in India used to say that if a tiger leaves the mountains and goes to the village, it will be hunted and die. But if it stays in the mountains among the pack, it'll grow and be healthy.

Look around you. Are your friends helping you grow and be healthy? Are they positive people? Are they encouraging your growth? Do they operate from a place of power or of love? These questions are important, because while our friendships can enable us to flourish, they can also keep us in our place.

I grew up in a small village where boys wore tracksuits. One day I came across a pair of flares, god knows where. I decided to wear them, and the suffering I experienced was enough for me to bury any trace of individuality I had for a decade. True friends will help you soar. True community will enable your change.

The old way of doing things is coming to an end, and a new way is coming in.

Community

Every few thousand years a Buddha appears, someone who meditates so diligently and precisely that they break right through the illusion of the mind and achieve enlightenment.

The last person to do this was Siddhartha Gautama. The story goes that after many years of trying different meditation techniques and reaching incredible levels of mental clarity, he had still failed to achieve enlightenment. So he developed his own practice. For seven days straight he meditated, and at the end of this period, he'd broken through the walls of the mind, and reached enlightenment.

But since Gautama died, a little over 400 years before the Christian era, there have been no Buddhas on the planet. Nobody has reached that level since.

Thich Nhat Hanh spoke about the next Buddha to come. He said it won't be one person, it might be an entire community.

The shift I believe we're all feeling at different levels right now is the shift towards loving community. This doesn't mean turning your back on people, but recognising the importance of real love, rather than convenience and opportunism, in the relationships that are closest to you.

The new community, I imagine, will be one based on true friends.

WHAT THE ALIENS CAN
TEACH US ABOUT LOVE

*'We think we know what a human being
should be but in the end all we know is
how a human can be in this paradigm.'*
—Pat McCabe

If you hadn't noticed, we are currently going through a
huge transition in the development of humans. Within
our lifetime, concepts like gender and sexual orientation
are being challenged to the point where they're becoming
irrelevant, and the patriarchy, capitalism and institutional
racism – great big words that have shaped and controlled
our lives – are being hounded and called out into extinc-
tion. My friends' children, the latest version of humans

on the planet, say things like they don't want to ever get married, or work for other people or limit themselves to the same gender restrictions that I grew up with.

We're on the brink of ushering in a new paradigm, a new way of being. Gently, in the background, especially for those who've selected automatic update permission, we humans are getting an upgrade. You can see it in the way the next generations are online. They're angry, and they're supposed to be. It's their job to tear down the habits and patterns we've established. That's why things feel particularly caustic in the world right now.

When we're older, we'll look back on this period as one of traumatic upheaval and revolution. We'll chuckle at the memory of how much changed in such a short period of time, and how many of us had to be broken, figuratively, to be built again. Our home is being renovated. Some people call this the birthing of a new Earth. The birthing part is why it appears like there's so much tension around us right now.

An equality omelette

As the author Caitlin Flanagan notes, if you want to make an equality omelette you have to break some eggs. We're making our relationships more equal too. If you listen carefully, you might hear the sound of the old ways cracking.

I have a vegan friend, who doesn't eat eggs, but who does channel aliens. I know, I left this bit of intel to near the end of the book, because I didn't want to lose too many readers, but I figure you're with me now.

She channels aliens. At least, she calls them aliens. You might call them guides. She tells me that we can all do this. We can all channel higher-dimensional beings, and in the future we will.

I ask her do they tell her lottery numbers, and she replies, 'No, Conor, stop being a prick.'

They do, however, give her visions of the future. Downloads, she calls them.

'Money will stop being a thing,' she says, 'because we'll understand that money is just energy, and we can create energy whenever we like. Power will be less attractive too. We'll understand that it's a burden, so nobody will want it any more.'

'Anything else?'

'Oh, we won't die. There are kids being born now who will live for ever,' the aliens tell her.

She describes the phase we're going through as a gradual process of awakening. It began a long time ago, but it is accelerating at the minute. Does time feel faster to you these days? Are realisations dropping more often? Are you doing things you never thought you would? Maybe she's on to something.

Buddha talked about the process of global awakening too. He illustrated it with a wheel. The wheel of dharma. The wheel started turning when Buddha gave his first talk after gaining enlightenment. We, as meditators, are invited to set this wheel in motion in our own lives. This is how we wake up, not just for us, but for the whole earth.

The new Earth that we are birthing, and to be fair, it couldn't come quick enough, is an Earth built upon fairness and maturity and awakened people. People who are awake not only in their lives but also in their relationships.

I ask my friend if the aliens think there will still be relationships in the future.

'Of course', she says, 'but they'll be very different.'

This is how our relationships might be, according to the alien wisdom of my friend.

Advanced trusting technology

You are your last authority on everything. Yes, we can discuss things with our friends, and we can read things in books, but ultimately our upgrade as a species is dependent upon us learning to trust ourselves. You will make your own decisions and you will make them based on the deep sense of knowing that comes from detaching from thoughts and trusting in presence.

We all get a glimpse of this. Our instinct is so much truer than we'd allow ourselves to believe. We can smell lies. We can taste authenticity. We can feel, just from the position of a person's body behind a microphone, whether they are speaking from their heart or their head. Our programming would have us believe that we're not really animals, that we don't really know these things.

The witch hunts that began in Europe and North America in the 1500s were primarily a way to eradicate this connection with our instinct. The witch hunts were a war against trusting in ourselves, and the legacy of this era still resonates in modern dating.

It's the point where we meet someone and we feel something's off, but we override the decision because logically they're a good match. And then, months later, years later, a whole friggin' lifetime later, children grown, empty nest, nothing but you, them and a TV screen, you'll think, *I knew something was up the first time we met, but I didn't do anything.*

In the future we will know, and we will trust that knowing. That's the big upgrade coming our way.

When you read wisdom, or hear some great advice, the only reason it resonates with you is because you already know it. Wisdom is open source. There's a great big collective databank of wisdom, and we access it when we operate from a place of presence. We just need to trust it.

Presence is our essential nature. It's our default state. The reason we don't trust ourselves is because we don't really know ourselves. We've become so disconnected from ourselves. We believe we are our thoughts; we believe we are our form. But this isn't us, this is just the old paradigm. Our ancestors believed that love was a form of ownership.

The new relationships on the new Earth will be founded on a sense of real love and real autonomy and real trust, and not fear-based patterns of enforcement. Future relationships will be based on knowing ourselves and making our own decisions. Our relationships will not be defined by what went before.

Maybe we won't live together, maybe we won't have children, maybe we won't be monogamous. Maybe our relationships will exist in a place of constant flux, held aloft by nothing more than a deep-rooted sense that we know what's best for us. Maybe we will be guided by heart wisdom and not the trauma in our bones.

Sure, you may not remember all your passwords, and you might need to rewatch crucial parts of movies to keep up, but you create the universe with the power of your mind.

You can trust yourself.

New security updates

The relationship models we've been handed down don't make us happy. Your grandfather probably didn't know anything about your grandmother's emotional or sexual needs. She probably didn't know much about his either. You can bet all your memories that they never had a conversation about polyamory. Relationship models of the past were built upon security. Sure, there was love, but when the knot was tied and the first child was born, it was mostly security.

In the future our relationships will not be built on a need for security, as we'll understand that our greatest source of security will come from inside ourselves. In the past, our relationship model was very much based upon this idea of what the other person has to offer. We were all essentially gold-diggers. And all our love was conditional. Our love was built on the lie of becoming and what will be.

The new love will be pegged to being and what is. It will be firmly linked to the present. Fear is rarely in the present. Fear is a part of our programming that causes us to experience near-constant worst-case-scenario simulations of the future. How will we afford this? What will my parents think? Where will we build our home? Love is very much right here and right now.

I write this, and at the same time I know full well that I don't always do this, but I'm trying. I think we're all trying, and I know that in the future we won't have to try as much, because our relationship with fear will have evolved.

Did you grow up with enough love? Most of us didn't. At least we didn't feel like we were loved enough when we were children. Yet despite that, we're still open to love, we still act lovingly, we still pick up books like these, even if a part of us might feel desperate or ashamed. Shifting our attention from fear towards love reveals to us a world that's actually full of love and loving gestures and loving people.

We are moving to a time when in all things, not just relationships, but our choice of clothing, how we travel, the work we do, is an opportunity to once again reject our education in fear and choose love. This is easy. The Earth we live on is really a hospital. A hospital for curing psycho-spiritual karmic disease. If you're here, then be cool, you've already got a highly sought after appointment. Now all you have to do is wait for the healing to begin.

In-house repairs

The attachment styles that we adopt when we get into relationships are much like the clothes we wear when we go on holiday: pinks, aquamarines, shawls, hats made from basket material. We dress like this because it sends a visual message to our minds – I am on holiday. *I am not at work, I am not at home, I am dressed impractically,* we say to our brains, *and with your permission, I'd also like to act impractically. Do you think you could give me a pass from worrying and being responsible for the next six days?*

Our attachment style is a little like an outfit that we wear when we find ourselves in a relationship. Beyond this one sticky realm, you might be independent, confident and immensely decisive, but put you behind the wheel of a WhatsApp chat with someone you're slowly connecting with, and you might become a mad person.

Insecure relationship patterns terrorise us. They keep us in an immature state. As one person's neediness triggers the other person's fear of responsibility, a perfect storm is created, with two otherwise sensible people becoming hurt and wounded, and anxiously waiting for the other one to change their actions and magically fix them.

This is important: We shouldn't go into relationships looking for people to fix us.

Your feelings are valid

… but they're not your partner's responsibility. They're all yours. And vice versa.

When our partners act out, or when they're sitting quietly at the end of the sofa, glued to their phone, we can allow them their feelings without always thinking, *Shit, they're mad at me.*

You have to walk the path on your own. Relationships are attractive because they appear at one level like a shortcut. As much as we might champion our freedom, we're also desperate to hand responsibility to someone else. Our hearts are like olive jars. Hey, I can't open this, can you try doing it for me?

*

I have always driven old cars. I believe that even if I were to be given a lot of money, a part of me would still want to only drive old cars. The problem, or if you want you could also call it the advantage, of driving old cars is that they are in need of constant care. Each trip to the mechanic, even if it's just to get an oil filter swap, is a little like a dash to the emergency room. I never know if they'll make it out again.

My mechanic knows me. Before fixing my car, he'll tell me exactly what's wrong with it. In this way, he gives me the option to proceed or not. Like my mechanic, your partner can tell you what's wrong with you, but they can't get under your hood and fix you. You're not a car, unfortunately. But this isn't a bad thing. In truth, we want our partners to have as little work to do as possible. We want it to be fun for them too.

Interdependence

Interdependence is a choice only independent people can make, writes Stephen Covey. Becoming independent simply means maturing. When we mature, we're ready for interdependent relationships.

When we love someone, we're offering them our friendship. This friendship doesn't deprive the other person of their freedom. In a relationship, not only are you intent on maintaining your own freedom, you're active in maintaining the freedom of the person you love.

We're growing. In a state of constant juggling and reinterpretation. Only our essence is fixed. Our essence is love, but our awareness of our essence is constantly expanding. The person who sent you kitten videos before you met them is not the same person you're sitting beside on the sofa months later. Our relationships change too. But more important, they are meant to change us.

Interdependence means recognising that we are all in the same boat together, but not sacrificing your own happiness so someone else can regulate their needs. Dependency is not love.

It's a by-product of our childhood that most adults want to be cared for by others. We want to transform our partners into ersatz parents, to make up for what we felt we lost as a kid. Marriage is a trap when we completely give up on an area of our development and hand over responsibility for that to our partner.

True interdependence is knowing that you could continue to survive and thrive without your partner, but choosing them as your partner anyway.

The wisdom of freedom

Love is not a binding contract; it should be voluntary. And all relationships should be open relationships. By that I mean open in the sense that neither person will feel controlled by the other, a relationship that has freedom at its foundation.

I write this with the full knowledge that there are many jealous bones in my body, but can I say I'm really loving if my focus is on preventing my partner from leaving rather than encouraging them to stay?

We can't force people to love us, but we try all the same. We use manipulation and guilt as mechanisms for governing our partner's behaviours. This is not a love based on giving, it's one where all we care about is receiving. We are a consumer society. Is it any wonder that we'd also consume people? Online dating has more in common with online shopping than it does with really connecting with real people.

To love as a fully awake, fully alive human is to love without the old rituals of security. To love fearlessly and free, that's our future.

Holding space

In relationships, not only do we get to suffer but we get to witness another person suffer, up close. This is not attractive. We find our way into relationships for somewhat superficial reasons: how a person smiles, how they dress, the way they talk to a waiter, their use of punctuation in a text message. And we find our way out of relationships for deeper, more inscrutable reasons: a person's attitude, their beliefs, how they kept bringing you down, how they never reached their potential and so on, and so agonisingly forth.

We come for the joy, but we leave for the misery.

But listen to this: nobody can bring you down if you are truly with your heart rather than your ego.

My father likes to play a game with my mother. He likes to ask her how she's feeling, out of ten. My mother always replies ten out of ten. This frustrates my dad. 'How can you always be that way?' he asks. My mum might be lying, but I don't think so. I think, no matter the circumstances, she's found a way to always feel ten out of ten. My mother, after years of struggle and work, now lives on a high-flying disc zipping its way across the sky.

*

Monastery life can be difficult, but it can also be relatively easy. There's drama in those quiet, airy spaces, but not nearly as much as in the real world. Living in the real world demands that we bear witness to it. Living with another person demands that we bear witness to them. If your partner's down, can you ask them what's up, or would you prefer to put on a movie?

If we truly love someone then our love's goal is to find the source of our loved one's suffering and help them. This is different from co-dependence, where we act out of need or obligation, or some insecure desire to control our partner. Holding space for our partner's suffering means recognising that your healing is intertwined. For you to become complete, you also have to grow in compassion.

That compassion doesn't mean you become a doormat: allowing bad behaviour is condoning bad behaviour. But compassion means holding space for another person's pain because their healing and yours move hand in hand.

Lifelong contracts

Lucretius was a poet from Pompeii, born less than a hundred years before Jesus. All that remains of him, apart from some statues here and there, is one poem. His poem was called 'On the Nature of Things', and in it Lucretius riffs about his philosophy. Much of it is to do with death.

'To fear death, then, is foolish, since death is the final and complete annihilation of personal identity, the ultimate release from anxiety and pain.'

Our relationships give us an insight into ourselves, but also into death and break-ups, when our contracts come to an end.

'Death ends a life, not a relationship,' says Morrie in the book *Tuesdays with Morrie*. If you think about your own life, no relationship truly ends. The effects, the ripples, continue long after you've parted ways, and will most likely continue to have their influence for many more lives to come.

Relationships could be the happiest part of our lives if we learned to let go of them when their time is up. Our break-ups are so fraught with anguish, when really all that needs to be said is that this doesn't make sense any more, let's let each other go.

We people addicted to pleasure stay unhappy for such long periods of our relationships. Often the reason we stay where we no longer want to stay is because there is a little part of us that believes we are actually bad, and undeserving. We need to get better at talking to ourselves. Telling ourselves that we are good.

When relationships end, as all things do, when people change, as all people do, we can move on with grace, kindness and the knowledge that we don't wait for love, we're constantly making it. We are phenomenally empowered, gifted beings of love.

Relationships are just habits. We are habitual creatures. We are consumed by our habits. They are obsessions. A relationship is an obsession. Monogamy is an obsession. Controlling people is an obsession. Chaos and order are the patterns that our world moves in – as do our relationships. If we want our relationships to grow, we have to be prepared to let them die and be reborn. This is realism.

Honest spirituality is invested in realism. I know I'm saying this at the end of a chapter that may or may not have been co-authored by aliens, but radical realism means examining your life, even its hard edges, and saying, OK, this is my conditioning, this is my programming, this is where I need to love myself, and this is where I need to trust myself, and maybe this is where I need to let someone go.

The people you really loved, you will love for ever, and nothing else really matters anyway. Don't worry about it so much.

BASIC DATING ADVICE, WITH NO WOO WOO

This shit's road-tested

I realise that a lot of this book has been a little on the cosmic side. I've spoken about past lives, future lives, other dimensions, states of consciousness, magic, and I've even talked up the idea that we're not really humans after all, more gods on vacation. (Yes, gods vacation on earth. They get an excellent group deal.)

Out of respect for those of you who might have picked up this book because you saw 'love' in the title but didn't realise the brew you were pouring into your cup: this chapter is for you. It's so practical that even your roommate, the guy who thinks you're a witch because you drink mint tea and listen to ambient music, could get down with it.

It's some condensed advice for dating. It's a run-down of some of the things I've learned from my own experiences. As a serial dater, I can assure you, this shit's been road-tested thoroughly. Most of it has emerged after the fact, often on long silent retreats, months after a break-up, licking my wounds and watching the pennies drop.

The most important thing to know when we're dating is that there are some rules.

Be kind to everyone

You can block, remove, ignore whoever you want in this world and still be kind to them. The reason I'm insisting that we all do our best to be kind is that we have no idea what type of battle each one of us is fighting on our own, but we do know that there is one, and it's fierce. The worst people in the world have to fall asleep at night too.

The other reason it's important to be kind is because one day you will die. And the people who you don't like will die too. And then, eventually – within 40 days, if the Buddhists are to be believed – you'll come back in another life. The person you weren't kind to will come back as well.

What if they're your mother? Or maybe they're your child? Or the person you attach to and marry (if marriage is still a thing in the future, I don't know), so just to be on the safe side, and to prevent any future awkwardness, let's be kind.

And let's be generous – and when I say generous, I mean genuinely generous – because giving is good for you. Giving turns the wheel of receiving. And let's forgive the people who have hurt us because we know that not forgiving, that hating and holding onto grudges are just ways to suck our energy and prolong our misery. Take an inventory of all the places where your energy is being sucked out, and you'll see there are opinions, beliefs and grudges that are causing the damage.

And the last rule: open your heart when you feel the giddy tingle in your chest, because regardless of what you've experienced and the trauma you've had, you know that hearts, like oyster shells, were meant to be opened, and so this is what you've got to do.

Turn all blames into one

This sounds about as much fun as cutting your hair with tweezers, but before you start mulling over other people's flaws – which is, honestly, what 99 per cent of dating is (the other 1 per cent being sharing subscription passwords for movie-streaming websites) – let's get this part clear: if you can't find some blame for your actions then you must be under some kind of spell. Shunryu Suzuki used to tell his students, 'Each one of you is perfect the way you are … and each one of you can use some improvement.'

We are far more perfect than we give ourselves credit for, but when it comes to dating, we place the burden for perfection not on ourselves, but on the other person. We have a tendency to expect things from others that we wouldn't readily give ourselves. This inevitably sets people up for failure, because no sooner do we start to get to know them than we also start finding things about them that annoy us. Whatever we dislike in other people, we can also find in ourselves. This doesn't mean that we lean into our inner asshole, but we do need to, at the very least, acknowledge that our inner asshole exists.

It's all on you

Look at the type of people you're attracting. It's no fluke. Your mind is the god of your little world. Depending on how well you train it, it can be a cute god who sends you job opportunities in Bali and emotionally mature partners, or it can be a despotic monster who keeps you chained to a desk until you're forced to resign because of burnout, only to be nursed by a partner who actually thinks, and makes no effort to hide, that you're faking it. This is your mind. If it shits all over the carpet and drinks from the toilet bowl, your mind is not broken, it just needs training.

We train the mind by becoming aware of it.

Think of the last time you went out into the world in a bad mood. Did you notice how that bad mood looked for fuel to keep burning? People annoyed you. Traffic was particularly intense. There was no toilet paper in the bathrooms at work. The deli guy buttered your bread, and you hate butter. You tune into social media and everyone's having a great time but you. You switch to the news and the world's on fire.

Your mind works a little like a bobsleigh. You point it in a direction and it will go there fast. When you wake up in a good mood, the world might still be in flames, but you also notice the good news stories. The commute is busy, but this morning you spot geese flying overhead in a V for- mation and, even though you're on public transport, you close your eyes and imagine what it might be like to fly, and this leaves you feeling giddy. So giddy that something comes over you and you chat to a guy in the line for coffee, and a voice speaks up that you didn't even know was yours and asks for his number. Look at you, you're a magician!

Bad and good moods are yours to choose from. And the people you attract are your choice too. It's not a matter of luck, it's a question of tendency.

You don't have a type, you have a habit.

Nobody can complete you, but they can show you how to complete yourself

If you look at the qualities in people you find attractive, they'll often lead back to the gaping holes in you. Anxious people seek out laid-back souls. Scaredy cats seek out brave adventurers. This is all well and good, but it's a short-cut. You cannot live by proxy.

I dated people who were creative, expressive, artists and musicians, because I wanted to be all those things. I imagined that, if I kept their company, some of their creativity would rub off on me. It didn't, though, because I invested all my time into supporting them. I paid bills, wrote their grants, made sure the fridge was full and tidied their studio spaces, but almost never created any art myself.

There's a lovely old expression concerning awakening. It's this: 'Don't confuse the telescope for the stars.' This means that yes, there are techniques and methods and groups and teachings, but don't forget what your end goal is. Your end goal is to get free, not just to meet people who are already free.

Endless curiosity

I've yet to meet a truly boring person. A problem with dating is that it tends to be so superficial that we don't get to know the other person. We meet strangers looking for them to entertain us. This is wildly unfair. Meet strangers with the intention of being the entertainer, of asking the questions, of taking the opportunity to sit with a fellow cosmic voyager and learn about their take on reality.

Each encounter with another human could bring with it the awe and mystery of cracking the seal on an ancient Egyptian tomb. Everyone has a superficial side and a deep side and, depending on your ability to make them feel heard and comfortable, you'll hear just the one.

Great expectations

Learning to critically judge your expectations can save you a lot of time. Like everything that goes on in our minds, our expectations are also illusions. In the future, as evolution drags us over the coals and forces us to mature, we'll see that we were wrong to expect things from other people.

In fact, if we'd got what we wanted, if we'd actually received what we expected, we'd never have understood that the world (in which we include people) is fundamentally unsatisfying. This process of being let down – repeatedly, if necessary – is pointing us towards an ultimate truth: You will never find anyone whose love is more important than your own. This leads us very nicely to the next bit.

Choose yourself

This doesn't always come naturally to us (it certainly didn't for me), but it's about as important as it gets. You need to put yourself first. You can call it a kind of conscious selfishness if you like. It's a way of moving out of your low-value programming. Most of us have this. We go out into the dating pool with a sense that nobody could love us. Yes, we make ourselves look, smell and even taste beautiful, but deep down, beneath the shimmer, we feel ugly, boring and unsuccessful.

Please don't go on a date if you feel like this. The most prominent noise in our heads is judgement, and this judgement rings like a bell, warning us of our past failings, our low potential, our darkest fears. It's just a channel that has caught our attention, and we can switch to another station. We are a people slowly wilting under tension and inadequacy. Choosing yourself is a radical thing to do. It means gifting yourself the things you want, doing what you want, asking for what you need and valuing yourself again.

Falling in love

There is something special about falling in love, but there's also nothing special about it at the same time. Falling in love is primarily about sex. When your body releases a deep moan as the object of your affection shuffles into view, it doesn't necessarily mean that you've encountered your soulmate – although it might – it mostly means that your hormones sense opportunity. Credit your hormones. They're the ones who are actually in charge. This pull to be close to a stranger is down to them. As a species, we'd be doing ourselves a huge service if we could admit that this mysterious, unquantifiable, magical and temporary spell at the beginning of any partnership is sexually motivated. *But they're different,* you'll protest, and maybe they are, but it's still sex. The longing is horniness. You're an animal.

This doesn't mean that falling in love is unstoppable, but it does remove some of its mystery and, thereby, hopefully, some of its allure. Falling in love is involuntary. We even sometimes fall in love with people who we don't really like. Opposites might attract sexually, but they rarely become close friends. From a spiritual point of view, falling in love is not your rocket ship to awakening. If anything, it involves a type of dulling of awareness. Two people, cheered on by their hormones, temporarily dumbing down for fun.

We look for love because we're lonely. We fall in love because of the dopamine flooding our brains. None of this is particularly useful to our deep spiritual development. A sugar high will not shatter the ego, after all. It's only after the falling in love stage that the real learning begins. Learning to love someone who our body has tricked us into loving through a cocktail of oxytocin is where our growing begins.

Do fall in love. Do lose your mind a little. Do eat up the illusion that some mysterious force has brought you and your date together. But don't let it distract from the real mystery: who are you when your thoughts, your programming and your hormones are not firing?

Don't take it so seriously

The more you can be aware of how much of your body's processes are conditioned responses based upon memories and impressions, the more you can relax into the experience. We are told from the youngest age that there is someone out there for us who we will love for ever. All we have to do is find them. *But how will I know?*, we ask the older people, who don't want to pass on bad news, so they reply with the unhelpful, avoidant brush-off, *Oh kid, you'll just know.*

The 'you'll know' part is confusing, because when we fall in love, I mean when the dopamine gates are opened, this feels like the moment everybody prophesied. This feels like the knowing, and so every time our brain lights up (and it can happen with a stranger in a bar, or a stranger online), we believe we've found the one.

I once met a date offline whom I'd known online for a few weeks. She texted beautifully. No typos, a great range of emojis, elegant shots of the dogs and cats she met throughout the first few weeks of online romantic blooming. I thought to myself, *Oh, this person is special.* She replied promptly, and asked questions of her own. We both liked flat whites, travel and reading. It was uncanny. After almost a month of online romantic bliss we met in real life for a drink, and, for both of us, it was the longest, most painful drink of our lives. Alone, with nothing but our imagination and our hormones to guide us, we'd created an illusion about each other. Now, finally brought together, we could see it for what it was: not a great match.

Seeing it for what it is is the hardest part of dating. It requires wisdom and awareness, and a bit of a ruthless streak. Recognising that something feels good but still walking away from it is a mark of discipline, but also of immense self-love.

Unbelievably, or perhaps expectedly, myself and that date went our separate ways, but we continued to text for months afterwards, even when we knew that there was no real future for us in the real world. The romantic myth is strong. Don't take it so seriously.

Balance the internal before exploring the external

If loneliness is the number one cause of relationships, it makes sense to put more work into your community rather than just one other lonely person. Many long-term relationships are based upon the slow whittling away of social connections, until the couple are isolated and even more dependent upon each other.

We have a belief that sticking to something is a mark of honour. This is why we stick at jobs that are killing us, or in places that no longer excite and in relationships where we are not understood, encouraged or inspired. Two lonely people will probably stay together for longer than two very independent people, but that doesn't mean they'll be any more satisfied or happy.

Question your reasons for looking for romantic love. And don't be too proud to acknowledge that loneliness is a factor, but don't think for a second that a romantic relationship is a cure for loneliness. I've met living saints who lived in caves for years and were so engrossed in the process of exploring their own minds that they never felt lonely for even a minute. Loneliness can be remedied through people, but it can also be explored through deeper, more intentional connection with yourself.

Change

'True love is born from understanding,' Buddha said. That also includes yourself. If you truly understood yourself, you would never believe the guilt, shame or judgement in your mind. When we break up with someone it can feel like a great treachery. Love has cheated us, or turned its back on us. We also run the risk of judging ourselves for the love seemingly falling apart.

But if romantic love is a myth, if the whole thing is an illusion, a conspiracy, if you like, backed up by your hormones and your culture, then when this kind of love breaks down you don't have to take it so personally. It's not your fault. Look at the other loves in your life. If you can manage to maintain love for your friends and your family (at least some of the time) then you're already pretty impressive at relationships.

The world, including you, is in a constant state of flux. In the future we'll recognise relationships for what they are: invaluable life lessons whose sole purpose is not to complete you, not to take away the pain and not to stop your growth, but to wake you up to the impermanent and unsatisfactory nature of life.

Love lasts for ever, but relationships don't have to

Just because a relationship lasts less than a few weeks that doesn't give it less worth. Longevity is no seal of quality when it comes to love. My favourite Italian expression is *Ama per sempre o finché dura*, or 'Love for ever or while it lasts'. It underscores what we know deep down to be true: our intention is to find love for ever, but the reality is, for the most part, wildly different. If you and your partner break up before one of you actually dies, then it hasn't been a failure on either of your parts. You can have a weekend with a stranger and share more vulnerability, more truth, more genuine caring than you might in a lifetime with a partner.

Your love is your own. You can give it, and you should give it to as many people as possible. Not just the folks who you are sexually attracted to, but to everyone. That love lasts for ever, but your relationships, especially if you want them to be places of caring, and effort and mutual growth, should be considered short-term ventures. If that short term gets continually extended, all the better, but so long as we keep the sense that we don't own our partners, that there's no cage for them to climb out of, that our relationships aren't closed, tied down, boxed off, but open and flowing and free spaces of honesty, tenderness and caring. This is how we marry romantic love and spiritual growth. This is how we grow up.

The future is a place where we meet our own needs, and we take responsibility for our own happiness. In this place our love pours out of us because we've learned to turn that switch on, and our relationships aren't sources of that love, or even contributors to it – more evidence that your love exists.

Work at it

This piece of advice might run contrary to the last, but there is so much to be said for sticking at something uncomfortable. Before you do this work, however, you really have to get right with your intention. Is this uncomfortable because you're growing, or is this uncomfortable because you're refusing to grow? Nobody can answer that question for you. You have to walk the path on your own and make the decisions on your own too.

This morning I went out for a coffee. If I'm working on a book I'm almost always out for coffee. Sometimes I drink too much and just type words like a maniac for an hour. Other times I drink too much and need to lie down. Much less often, I'll be inspired. This morning I was inspired by a couple who were fighting in the line before me. Initially I could feel it. Her body language was all sharp and animated and prickly. If she'd been covered in hair, it would most certainly have been standing up on end. He was all slumped over like he was looking for pennies at his feet. I immediately thought, right, here's another example of why it's so important to get better at breaking up with people. I was lining up for my oat milk flat white – reusable cup in hand – with a smug sense that whatever I was doing with my coffee habit, this book was on the right track. I looked at them with a feeling of superiority.

And then, she did something I didn't expect. She reached out a hand and put it on his shoulder, then said, 'Sami, this is something you always do.' And Sami shuffled a little, looked up from the floor and smiled at her and said, 'You know me so well.' 'Of course I do,' she replied, and she kissed him on the forehead.

Our society teaches us that love is a neurotic, co-dependent dance of security, much like geopolitics and the dance of superpowers. But love and our relationships can also be as simple as just getting to know someone to the point where they cease to frustrate you and begin to fascinate you.

SEX

'Intimacy is the capacity to be rather weird with someone – and finding that that's OK with them.' —Alain de Botton

Sex is all about connection and acceptance – with other people, but mostly with yourself. Your body, its pleasure, the way it responds and rejoices when it's close to another. What it can do, the levels it can reach, how good it can feel.

Good sex can actually change your physiology. The neural rhythms of good sex can drop us into trance-like states. Some folks believe that orgasms cleanse the body and release energy blockages, traumatic blockages, the bugs in our system. Good sex rubs off, spills over and leaks – ahem, drips – into every other part of our lives.

When I'm out drinking coffee on a Sunday morning, I like watching people on their way home alone or going for breakfast after a night together. It's no walk of shame, more a swagger of triumph. Someone who's had good sex looks taller, lighter, more fluid with their movement. They order extra eggs from the waiter. They are truly in their being, and they are hungry.

Sex can bring us back to life. Couples who've been floating apart for many months or years can suddenly, at a wedding, after a tragedy, on the fullest of full moons, fall into some accidental love-making and rediscover the connection that hooked them in the first place.

So much we've talked about in this book has been the way our conditioning, our programming, our karma and the society around us are constantly trying to disconnect us from ourselves. Ever been riddled with doubt, self-hate, worry about your appearance, the things you say and said? Well, that's your proof that the disconnection is working. You are being pulled apart.

Our sex is often disconnected too. It can make us feel inadequate or shameful. Sex can be very unsexy. The sex we have that should and could expand us can make us feel small and unattractive and depleted. Don't take it personally; take it collectively.

Sex, love, intuition and feminine power have all been mistreated and devalued by the patriarchal society we collectively live in. Naturally, our sex is not as satisfying as it could be. If the tree's poisoned, so's the fruit. Sex can be an ecstatic journey into transformation. As people we need to rebuild our relationship with intimacy and learn to use sex as a ritual for healing and connection.

Sex is vulnerability

It is no measure of health to be well adjusted to a profoundly sick society. Jiddu Krishnamurti said that. I read it at a time in my life when I was in a relationship with someone who didn't want to have sex with me any more. We were completely disconnected. We had had a very active sex life, and now, six months or so later, we would lie together in bed, and while she slept, I'd stare at the ceiling and feel frustrated.

I knew she was frustrated too, but we didn't talk about it. Neither of us was enjoying our intimacy any more, but to talk about it, to bring it out into the open, would have been so painful and awkward for both of us that instead we picked fights about other things.

The problem with our sex life was our problem with vulnerability. Real intimacy goes far beyond what we do with our bodies and asks us to strip back the layers of armour that we have around our hearts.

With different skills, we might have turned to each other and said, *Hey, I don't really care about all that, right now I just don't feel loved, held or seen by you. Do you think we could just slow down a little and address this?*

But of course we didn't slow down. As our relationship worsened, our need to be busy grew until we were both frantic, coming and going at all times, catching each other over breakfast, missing each other at weekends, talking mainly over WhatsApp, sad emoji faces, pictures of solo meals, Post-its on leftovers in the fridge.

'Our hurry and embarrassment look ridiculous,' Ralph Waldo Emerson said, talking about modern life.

Sex is divine

Love is action, but sex, the ultimate example of teamwork, is communication. The reason we're having sex with each other isn't just for pleasure, but ultimately to bring more love into the world. We bring more love into the world by recognising ourselves and then seeing our self in everyone else we meet.

Sex is a form of recognition. An elaborate nod of the head. A very enthusiastic handshake. Even if it's just you at home alone with a scarf over the lamp, sex is the release of a deeply powerful loving energy of appreciation. We know this and want this intuitively, but our intellect, our identification with the sea of thoughts and memories that comprise our intelligence, gets in the way of our intimacy.

In original Hinduism, they teach that sex is divine. Lama Yeshe was a Tibetan teacher who lived for a time in California. He said this:

> It is precisely because our present life is so inseparably linked with desire that we must make use of desire's tremendous energy if we wish to transform our life into something transcendental.

Christian puritanism changed so much of this for me. The heavy weight of shame associated with sex in most parts of the world today is a bit like a collective trauma. It's a karmic weight. They took sex from us and told us it was somehow a bad thing.

It wasn't until I was well into my thirties that I was introduced to the idea of sex as a planned event, a ritual, rather than just something that happened at the end of a night out, or on my own as a form of stress relief.

Sex is potential

We can unlock the magic of the moment by being present with our lives, and we can do the same with sex. Sex is the most creative act. In some cases it creates life, in others it creates a merging of people, a rare opportunity to see yourself in another. A way of collapsing ego boundaries.

We are busy, but we're also afraid of vulnerability, afraid of our own potential and our own desire. Sex is a lot like a dormant force inside us.

I have a mysterious wooden object on my desk. It fits in your hand and is perforated with small holes. I don't know how it ended up in my home. It must have been a gift. I tried using it to hold pens, but most of the pens were too fat for the holes, so instead I'd use it as an incense holder. One day, a friend was over, and we were both seated at the desk. She picked it up, shook it free of ash, and then, putting it between her lips, made the most beautiful music with it.

'What is that?'

'It's an ocarina,' she said. 'It's an instrument.'

'I never knew.'

She played some kind of campfire music, and readers, as opposed as I typically am to campfire music, it sounded like the music my soul might make when it finally winds its way home.

There's something of the ocarina in all of us. We're sleeping giants, dormant forces, fierce dogs afraid of our own barks. Sex shines a spotlight on this.

Sex is acceptance

How do you feel about your body? Our shame around sex is so often connected to our shame around our body.

Buddha gave a sermon on the idea that our bodies are gross. He called it the Satipaṭṭhāna Sutta. In it he goes into great detail about what happens to our bodies after we die, and how various other beings, from vultures right down to worms, devour these bodies that we think so much about. The point of the sermon was not to turn us against ourselves, but to provoke our curiosity: what animates your body?

My relationship with my body has never been easy. Chicken legs, milky-white skin, teeth fighting to get away from each other. Sex, those magical healing moments when someone chooses to get close to your naked body, taught me to slowly accept myself.

It took many partners and a lot of loneliness to learn that I could also turn myself on. To learn to ask for things in the bedroom. Can you touch me there? Could you do that? Can I do this? Simple things that came out of my mouth at the speed of cold molasses.

I worked for many years in bars and clubs in Berlin. In one club there was a guy who hung out in the men's bathroom. He was very polite, very sweet and would gently ask other men to pee in his mouth. Most of them obliged. People called him the pee goblin. He was kind of well-known. I don't know what happened to the pee goblin when he wasn't in clubs. Maybe he had a desk job. Maybe he had a family. I don't know whether he was healthy or not, and I don't think it's my position to judge. But I do know that even he could ask for what he wanted. Perhaps that's something to think about.

We are weird little beings in a very narrow and confining world. Sex can be our playground. A place where we tease, tickle, touch, lick and even pee on ourselves and others. Sex can be a place where we finally accept ourselves, in all our weird, kinky glory.

Bodies aren't beautiful. What bodies do is beautiful.

Sex is good, actually

For a Buddhist, life's purpose is working your karma. Karma is a type of spiritual gravity that binds us to the suffering of the world. Our karma, the accumulation of what we have done over many, many lives, is what we're working through right now. It's why you are born where you are and in the form that you are. Our karma is our relationship with our self, with our bodies, and with sex.

I believe that mine will be one of the last generations of humans born on the planet to grow up not talking openly about sex. I hope that I'll be one of the last generations to require Dutch courage in order to be sexually expressive. We will be comfortable with vulnerability because we will understand that vulnerability leads to better sex. In my time we believed that aftershave and perfume led to better sex.

Our relationships could be easy. Two independent people who know how to self-soothe and self-pleasure coming together for the purpose of exploring love and themselves through vulnerability, acceptance and the powerful dormant forces inside their bodies.

When we do have sex, it bridges the gap that separates people, but also in those seconds – or, here's hoping, minutes – when you are deeply present, it bridges the gap that separates you from the divine.

Intimacy is like an ocarina. The instrument is said to be more than 12,000 years old. It looks simple. Even a little ugly. You learn it intuitively. Pick it up and blow. There are no bum notes. Put your fingers where you want to. See what sounds and feels good to you. Play the greatest-sounding music you can – accept whatever comes out, love it, protect it, cherish it, just don't let it gather dust on your writing desk.

Part 5
Us

LOVE AS A FORCE FOR CHANGE

'You are born alone. You die alone. The value of the space in between is trust and love.' —Louise Bourgeois

We're all born with broken hearts. Just this being human means to own a heart that is somehow faulty. It feels too much. It hurts too quick. It shuts off entirely, for years even, powering briefly back on when we hear Adele or, in my case, Nico, playing on the radio. Man, can it be sensitive, overwhelmed on its birthday, bursting into tears after two glasses of wine, snapping at people who ask with no malice or ill intention, *Are you OK in there?*

This little life, and this little broken heart. Broken but still functioning, like a machine that's long run out of fuel but can still generate a bit of forward movement from the fumes. Look at it go. Look at your own heart go, busted, battered, one harsh look away from near annihilation, yet unstoppable at the same time. Your heart is unstoppable. You are unstoppable.

Alice Walker wrote: 'The way forward is with a broken heart.'

So here we are with all our broken hearts on planet Earth. Sometimes it's a lot of work, right? See, this place is a school. We come here to learn about ourselves. You learn what you like, what you don't like. You learn how you like to be touched, how you don't like to be touched. You learn the rhythms of your broken heart. You see how it plays with others. Some make it dance, some make it hurt even worse. Much worse. Some make you wish you never had a heart at all.

This is very normal. Our journey takes us first away and then finally back to our hearts, because they're not really broken after all. They just appear that way. We've been trying to operate for thousands and thousands of years with hearts that aren't fully open. Picture a bird trying to fly without opening its wings. It would belly flop on every branch. That's how we've been loving for all these years. This is why we hurt.

As you do away with your old conditioning and accept yourself, your heart begins to open. An open heart is the most powerful thing on this planet.

We're on earth to learn how to open these hearts of ours. We're learning that, despite all the songs, all the poetry, all the movies and all the stories passed down in our genetic memory, our hearts aren't so much broken as just not opened correctly. We need to open our hearts and harness the remarkable energy they possess. This is our future, and it's coming fast.

Love is a superpower

There's a thing I've been doing for the past two years. It grew from a broken heart. My broken heart left me feeling lonely. Good things grow from loneliness. Loneliness is an invitation to act. Loneliness can be the beginning.

It was winter, long nights, cold-ass mornings, and I found myself living alone again and feeling it deeply. Being alone has always been a challenge for me. I don't mind it at first, but after too long on my own I begin to grow in weird ways. I get a little spooked by company. All invitations to socialise feel like burdens to bear. I don't stop washing, I don't pace around my home barking, I don't smear the walls in paint, but I do become a little weird. What happens to you when you're alone for too long? How weird do you get?

If you notice that you are repeatedly returning to loneliness, then listen very carefully. Maybe the loneliness wants to tell you something. Maybe it has some intel just for you. This is what the loneliness told me:

You can send waves of love through your own body, at any time, in any situation, on good hair days or bad, and it costs nothing. So this is the thing I've been doing. I wake up, and before I open my eyes, before I meditate, before I even go and pee, I'll just lie there sending waves of love from my heart down to my toes, out along my arms and up to my head. If someone were to walk into my room and say, *Conor, are you sleeping?* I'd say, *No, I'm pumping my body full of love, can I get a little peace in here?*

It's strange, because I describe it as me sending love, like I'm a great big engine churning love out of my heart with the power of my clumpy, supersized brain, but the reality is I don't believe I'm doing much at all. When I pay really close attention, I see that I'm not activating love, I'm simply not blocking it any more. You don't have to do much to allow love, you really just have to do less. The love's there all the time just waiting for you to drop your guard.

You can send waves of love through your own body, at any time, in any situation, on good hair days or bad, and it costs nothing.

This old broken heart is just waiting to open as soon as you take your foot away from the door.

If you're reading this book, then you are in the process of opening your heart. This I'm certain of. You wouldn't have got this far if you weren't. That's not to say that if you don't like certain things from the spiritual world that you're simply not ready for them. There's a lot of junk out there, after all. You don't need to be scared of it. You are your own authority. You can trust your own taste.

But if parts of this book are resonating with you, then you're almost certainly in the process of transformation, and the world will be changing around you. You'll be growing more sensitive. Your heart will be opening. Your chest might be tingling. Love will be growing inside you, and you might be wondering what to do about it. Should I see a doctor? Should I quit dairy? How many glasses of water a day will all this new love need?

Answer: Eight will do.

Try it. Right now, send waves of love from your heart down to your toes, out along your arms and up to your head and see if you can feel anything.

The anti-love agenda

As your heart opens, you might find yourself wondering, What in the world next?

Gloria Steinem said that the final stage of healing is using what happens to you to help other people.

The final stage of your healing process is healing others. Our society is loveless, but humans are loving. Deeply loving. Grind or die is not our way, but somehow it's become that. What kind of drunken mess were we in when we signed up for five days a week? I know far too many people who deny their body sleep, nutrition, fresh air and joy in order to make ends meet. I do it too. We all do.

Capitalism, the story that governs how we live on this planet, is a mostly loveless system designed to disconnect us from ourselves and ultimately from love. It's spikes in the concrete so homeless people can't overnight, it's designed obsolescence, it's social media leaving everyone feeling that their bodies aren't good enough, and it's the world of dating, where we're slowly losing the most important aspect of new companionships: tolerance for each other's differences.

Modern dating is often cruel.

I left Dublin when the magazine I wrote for went bankrupt and my landlord increased our rent in the same month. I moved to Berlin because at the time it felt like a less cruel city. You could work three nights a week as a bartender and survive. There were shops run by punk collectives that gave things away for free on the understanding that you would, in brighter times, donate what you could. I still own a T-shirt that I got in that shop, and in return I've given them about three vacuum cleaners that were no longer up to the task of sucking cat hair out of the carpets. Thank you, planned obsolescence. Communal free meals, known as Volksküche, could be found in every squat, and back then there were plenty of squats. You could eat for free, and even though I didn't need to eat for free, it was a huge comfort to know I could.

But the cruelty reached Berlin too. Berlin, like most cities, is being strangled by wealthy developers. Many of my friends are forced to move home every six months or so because long rental contracts are so hard to come by, so expensive, so cruelly designed to strip renters of their rights. Cruelty is everywhere. The anti-love agenda is relentless.

Kindness is all around

Love is stronger than hate, and we as people are more loving than we're given to believe.

Kurt Vonnegut, the writer, wrote a message to any new-comers who might visit our planet, 'Welcome to Earth,' he said, 'you just have to be kind.'

I see kindness everywhere, and it feels like a movement to me. A few years back I had to explain to people what meditation is, and now everybody's explaining it to me. Folk talk about energies now. My dad understands the power of forgiveness. More and more I'm having conversations with strangers about the positive and mysterious changes taking place in their lives.

Alpha males are in couples therapy. Workaholics are quitting their jobs. We drink less. A meal without meat can still be a meal. We're evolving beyond what we see and hear to understand the world at a sense level, at the level of feelings. The media would have you believe that the world is a box divided into good or bad, but my world is a place of forgiveness and kindness and growing understanding.

PEACEFUL
REVOLUTIONS

'Rebellion cannot exist without a strange
form of love.' —Albert Camus

'I think there's a weapon of cynicism to
say, "Protest doesn't work. Organising
doesn't work. Y'all are a bunch of hippies.
You know, it doesn't do anything",
because frankly, it's said out of fear,
because it is a potent force for political
change.' —Alexandria Ocasio-Cortez

Make love, not war

If you're feeling down about your life right now then maybe it's not about you, but about the structures we live in. If you're renting a shitty spot to pay off someone else's mortgage, adhering to unloving relationship models because you've been programmed with guilt and shame, doing a joyless job because there are for the most part only joyless jobs, and spending your money on devices that make you dumb and miserable and addicted, then maybe you're not the problem, the structures are.

We are loving beings. When we are in balance, we are more compassionate than competitive, and until the structures we live in reflect that, we'll always feel down about our lives. It's not you, it's it.

And in order for *it* to change, we all need to become activists. Loving activists.

There's one activism that takes place in public, and another that takes place in private. There's the activism that takes to the streets and demands change from the dominant culture that governs our lives, and there's an activism that gets alone, gets very quiet and explores the dominant conditioning in ourselves.

If we are to bring care, respect, trust, commitment and love into our society and our institutions, we'll need both.

Corporate power doesn't love you, but let's face it, often you don't even love yourself.

Join the revolution

As above, so below. As below, so above.

The external world is a reflection of the internal world. If you're encountering bullies in the outside world, are you also maybe bullying yourself internally? If you're running down dead ends in your bid to build a life for yourself, are you also maybe not giving yourself a chance?

How loving is your internal world? Are you at peace even some of the time? Do you prioritise your needs? Do you allow yourself to dream? Do you choose loving relationships? Are you reacting compulsively to the world as it hits you, or are you responding consciously? Who controls whom?

You see, the world shapes human consciousness. As above, so below. Meanness creates more meanness. Fear sparks more fear. If someone fucks you over, you might be more inclined to do it to the next person. And if someone dumps you hard enough, you will engineer each future relationship so that it's you doing the dumping this time. You will seal your heart shut, and good luck to whatever dreamboat comes along, they won't get through.

But if it can be one way, it can also be the other. As below, so above. Human consciousness can shape the world. Your being is just as important as your doing. Your example can be your activism.

'Give light and people will find the way,' says Ella Baker.

When I watch the news, or read about the environment, or learn another insane detail about the billionaires who play with our futures, it can make me angry. But if you're angry you've already lost. Holding on to anger is like grasping a hot coal, Buddha said. You are the one who gets burned. If you open your heart enough it can and will dissolve your anger.

I never imagined I'd be able to share a table with my father and not only feel comfortable around him but also feel love and respect for all he has done for me. I consider that a miracle. The last time we spoke on the phone I mentioned that I was feeling lonely. Later he sent me a message with the most beautiful words I'd never imagined possible: 'If you're ever feeling lonely again, call me. I'm here for you.'

Your love can, if you let it, take all your private hurt away. It can also take our collective hurt away.

The deep longing at the core of your being is to open your heart, despite your pain, and expand limitlessly. This is also the deep longing of your enemies, and the people who have done you wrong – even, although you might find this hard to believe, your bosses, your bullies, the people who attack you.

Liam Gallagher said that he was going to start a revolution from his bed. The idea that we can start a revolution wherever we are right now, even in our beds, is solid. We can start revolutions on our own.

How? Love yourself

You have the power to create the things you believe. You can create any world you choose. If you, like me, dream of a more loving, caring world, then we don't necessarily have to collapse greedy corporations, dethrone politicians and ground military jets at the airports; we can also simply open our hearts and start creating happiness around us.

If you can begin to create happiness in your own life, and the lives of everyone you meet – not a soft or easy task by any means – you will eventually and dramatically change the world. Make peace with your neighbours, forgive your parents, drop the grudges you hold towards your old lovers, your old schoolmates, your old employers. Come together. Don't be divided. Love everyone.

When we rage against the machine, we're not talking so much about the hollow institutions that symbolise power on this planet, we're talking about the illusion of division between people. We're all alike, you and me. Awareness shows us that. By putting out the fire of anger and resentment inside yourself, you will begin to extinguish the roaring flames of hurt in the world.

All our lives we're tricked into believing that love is something you can buy, find or achieve, and that the only effective way to deal with those who wrong us is to hate them. The most powerful people in our societies encourage this trick because it's good for sales. Division creates demand.

If you don't like the society around you, and you'd like to change it, the most radical thing you can do is learn to love yourself and forgive everyone. A loving rebellion could be as simple as everyone practising forgiveness and acceptance. An uprising of open hearts.

THE FUTURE

'You are recycled butterflies, plants, rocks, streams, firewood, wolf fur, and shark teeth, broken down to their smallest parts and rebuilt into our planet's most advanced living thing.' —Aubrey Marcus

Buddha was all love

Buddha travelled non-stop through India teaching anyone who wanted to learn. According to the sutras, he gave over 100 talks, which would have meant he was delivering the equivalent of at least two and even three TED Talks every day. How did he do it? He was helped by love.

One story goes that right at his death – a death he had predicted down to the day, of course – the guy was already halfway out when someone requested a meeting with him. Eyes closed, shallow breaths, inches from the pearly gates, and someone walks up to the crowd paying respects to his body and says, 'I need him to teach me how to meditate.' Buddha's followers tried to shoo the guy away. 'Come on, man', they said, 'can't you see he's about to pass from this life? We'll teach you tomorrow, come back then.'

But the guy begged. 'He's the real deal, and I'm this close to him. I don't want you to teach me. Let me learn from him.' Buddha, hearing this, waved his soon-to-be-cold hand and ushered him over. 'This man has come to the Ganges', he told his assistants, 'let him drink.'

Buddha was all love. He knew that awakening and community go hand in hand. What's the point in seeing through the delusion of self, solving the Rubik's Cube of misery and discovering that the world pours out of you, not towards you, and not having anyone to talk to about it?

You are made of love

The people who know me, my family, my close relationships, they know I've been meditating a lot when they get cute messages from me in the early morning. 'I appreciate you. I'm so happy you're in my life. I love you.' You get the gist. The tiny glimpses of awakening that I stumble upon in meditation, and the moments in my day when I can bring more presence, charge me with a sense of love and optimism that I'm compelled to share.

To be born into a human life on planet Earth is a remarkable stroke of luck. It's a prize already won. Simply being here at this explosive, chaotic and transformative time is a kind of victory. It is our responsibility to create a more awakened, more loving society here.

If you feel love you want to share it. Love's purpose is to grow inside you and eventually bloom in your words and actions. If we want a more loving world, we can just be loving ourselves. The rest will fall into place.

I know how ridiculous that might sound. It wasn't so long ago that I was hounding drunks out of bars, cleaning puke from thick carpet and arriving home most nights at 2am with a cold sandwich and a carton of orange juice (I was, in my own way, trying to be healthy) with very little hope for myself or the planet. I didn't imagine I could be happy or have dreams of being a microcosm of love. I would have most definitely laughed at myself. I would certainly have considered myself a bit soft.

The path of love is pretty much a path of faith. If I'm feeling love, it's personal. I can explain it to people around me, but it's always somehow disappointing. Words don't do it justice. This book has about 50,000 of the little things, and they won't do it justice either. My hope is that, at the very least, they'll make you feel more empowered. That they will help you trust and then wait for the rest to fall into place.

We are taught that love is something that comes to us. It is out of our control. That's a lie. This lie is the number one cause of misery and negativity on our planet. You are made of love. It comes out of you like sweat beads come out of your head when you have a fever. Your purpose in life is not to get rich, get married or have children – your purpose in life is to simply discover the love inside yourself and enjoy it in whichever way you choose.

HOW TO ACTUALLY
LOVE EVERYONE

Be tolerant

Our learning comes because of and with other people.
People exist not to give us love, but to show us how we
might be more loving. Everyone is an opportunity to move
a little closer to expanding our hearts and approaching our
true destiny. People are our teachers, especially the ones
who get under our skin.

I'm writing this final chapter at the house of two
lovely friends who live on Mallorca. We're spending winter
together. They have kittens here. Sometimes the kittens
fight. Sometimes they get into the worst ruckus and wake
us all up. We'll run down the stairs and find a bottle of

olive oil spilling across the kitchen floor and a poop in the middle of the table.

The kittens are learning how to be tolerant of each other. They're learning how to share. It's not always easy for them. On some days they curl up in a tight bundle, heads over tails, paws wrapped tightly around each other, and on other days it's a battlefield of oil and tiny shits.

Living with my friends is also a learning exercise. We cook together, we share space together and we try to communicate, with great and sometimes awful diplomacy, our needs as little humans. We are practising tolerance and hoping that it won't get to the stage where we're making a mess in the kitchen.

I haven't always been so tolerant in my life, but tolerance is something you can learn. It's something I've been learning. Becoming tolerant is how we finally grow up and at the same time grow closer to people.

'Love is our true destiny,' Thomas Merton said. 'We do not find the meaning of life by ourselves – we find it with another.'

Do as Buddha does

Buddha knew this. He knew that our destiny as people was to grow more tolerant of each other. Buddha didn't leave us hanging. Buddhism has a pathway in place. The Four Immeasurables, as they are called in Buddhism, are four states of mind that we can all practise. They are the Buddhist guide for making friends and loving people. They are: equanimity, love, joy and compassion.

In a hundred years' time, the habit pattern of our minds will no longer be fear, scarcity, resentment and obligation, it will be the Four Immeasurables. But by practising this now, much like the folks who bought Bitcoin in 2009, you're getting a head start. You will, when the time comes, be loaded.

Be calm

Everyone, even your ex, just wants to be happy. Or, as a good friend once told me after I'd been stood up, 'Mate, she wipes her arse like everyone else.' Everyone you meet is simply acting out of a desire to be content, safe and healthy. Bad behaviour is not endemic to humans; it's a reaction to when we are engulfed by fear. If a person truly loves themselves, they can't hurt other people. Recognising this can help us deal with other people.

Be loving

Don't you want your ex to be happy? How much better would your life be if everyone, even the pricks in your life, were healthy and safe and happy? It's in your own self-interest for everyone to feel love. And anything you can do to enable those around you to feel loved leads us to the logical conclusion that it makes sense to try to love everyone.

Be kind

Everybody hurts. Can we move beyond our own pain and recognise the pain in others? Nobody gets out of life without some pain, regardless of the details.

Trauma has less to do with what happened and more to do with how you felt while it happened. A good friend of mine lived through the siege of Sarajevo as a child. He watched a neighbour get shot in the street outside his window, but he tells me that he doesn't remember it as a traumatic time, because he spent all three years of it in the close company of his mother and his friends, hiding out together, playing card games and singing songs. He felt protected despite the circumstances. He felt loved and free to express himself.

Another friend of mine grew up in a seemingly perfect home. Her parents didn't drink, didn't fight, they visited Disneyland, got all the right dentistry and never felt hungry or scared once, yet she is riddled with deep fears. She's scared of water, scared of certain foods, she doesn't want to stay alone in her house. She's always anxious in relationships. It would be easy to dismiss her concerns based on the evidence, but what we feel is what we then take to be true.

Compassion for others means recognising that what someone feels is valid. Compassion means instead of labelling a person as bad, we can recognise that they're in pain and that their pain is causing them to behave badly.

Be joyful

Scarcity and fear create division. They make us want to compete with each other. Life is not a race, it's a choir. We're not trying to win, we're just trying to sing a tune together.

Often when our friends succeed, when they get the job, they get the wedding ring, they get the winter holiday while you're freezing your arse off in a sublet where the shower takes ten minutes to get warm in the morning, we feel resentment. This is the lesson of scarcity. Scarcity teaches us that there's not enough fortune to go around.

The opposite of scarcity is abundance: the sense that if someone else can achieve it, well so can I. We humans are playing on the same team. If one wins then why can't we all win? The conditioning we learn in school and in our societies is that our lives are a competition for survival. This concept doesn't hold any weight. The defining elements of a human is our ability to communicate and our ability to trust. That's what got us out of our little caves and into spaceships.

An advantage gained is not an advantage lost. We all go up together. The habit of the fearful part of our brain is to see fortune as a limited stock; the loving part of our brain knows that there's enough to go around.

GROWING TOMATOES ON A NORTH-FACING BALCONY IN BERLIN

At night, the kittens sleep outside the house. This is what they're used to, and where my friends live it doesn't get so cold at night. We built a little mountain of cushions for them in an outside toilet. The kittens climb in together because they know that bodies heat bodies. Many animals rely on each other for thermoregulation. Penguins do it. They cluster together in the cold.

Once upon a time we did too. Perhaps half of all sexual desire is really just the wish to be close to another warm body. The history of humans is a history of starving, freezing and being eaten alive. Before we were top of the food chain, we weren't far off the bottom.

In the time before central heating, sushi at your door in 30 minutes or less, and fierce animals on Netflix rather than on our trail, we depended on each other for everything.

We still do. Your happiness and wisdom come to you through your relationships. If you pass a homeless person on the street, and you're sensitive to it, you'll notice the pain inside you. If you see a stranger crying on a park bench, your heart might ache a little.

What happens to other people, even those we don't know, affects us. So love everyone. It sounds soft. It might even sound a little Hallmarky. But it's one of the bravest things you'll ever attempt. Equanimity, love, compassion and joy are a type of quadrathlon of the heart. It's daunting.

If we look very carefully, we can imagine a beautiful world in the future. We don't know how to get there yet, but we do know it's there, and if we can bring it into existence in our hearts then, one day, not too far away, we'll also bring it into existence in our hands.

I've resisted using too many analogies in this book. We writers about meditation have a habit of doing that. We talk about the clouds, and we talk about the sea. We compare thoughts to the setting sun, our existence to the life of a butterfly, sometimes we get quite carried away, so I've resisted. But let me, at the death, try one.

We are gardeners.

I don't know why, perhaps it's because I'm now in my forties and most of the fun and games and high drama that I've written about in this book are behind me, but gardening appeals to me a little more. Mucky fingers fill me with joy. I grew tomatoes last year on a north-facing balcony in Berlin. Every day I'd go out and look at them growing with a sense of wonder. Starved of light, downwind of two traffic-heavy streets, in a handful of muck and cat dung, these tomato plants had shot towards the sky. They are very special tomatoes.

Loving everyone would be easier to do in a lighter world, and tomatoes would be easier to grow in brighter conditions, but the sense of satisfaction earned from attempting what you think is impossible and finding out it's possible cannot be matched. There are 8 billion people on this planet and, for better or for worse, you are in a relationship with every single one of them.

You are special. Your opinion matters. Your time is important. There is something beautiful growing inside you, and it's love. Trust it. Tend to your needs. Be a constant gardener of your heart, because the love that is growing in you can change you, and then the whole world.